# FIRST STEPS TO FREEDOM

*By the same author:*

Autohypnosis
Creative Visualization
Advanced Autohypnosis

# FIRST STEPS TO FREEDOM

## Achieving Non-attachment in Everyday Life

RONALD SHONE

Aquarian/Thorsons
*An Imprint of* HarperCollins*Publishers*

The Aquarian Press
An Imprint of HarperCollins*Publishers*
77 – 85 Fulham Palace Road,
Hammersmith, London W6 8JB

Published by The Aquarian Press 1991
1  3  5  7  9  10  8  6  4  2

A CIP catalogue record for this book
is available from the British Library

ISBN 1-85274-092-2

Typeset by Harper Phototypesetters Limited
Northampton, England
Printed in Great Britain by
Mackays, Chatham, Kent

# Contents

# Preface

I am not sure when this book was conceived. For some years I had been reading esoteric literature, and in particular in the last few years the works of Gurdjieff and his followers. More recently I began to read the Spanish mystics, and I was struck immediately by the similarity of what they had to say on the topic of non-attachment. Although the former works talked of *non-identifying*, while the latter talked of *detachment*, it was quite clear that they were referring to the same phenomenon. Some other writers talked of *non-attachment*, which appeared to me to be a much better term. From these beginnings I began a more thorough search of what various writers had to say on the subject.

In this search a second feature struck me most forcibly. Although a number of writers argued that non-attachment was very important for human development, especially spiritual development, few gave any clear explanation of why this was so and, more importantly, how to achieve it. Once I began to ask the question 'What is non-attachment?' I found it very difficult to answer. My explanation made people think too readily of detachment – and if not detachment, certainly self-centred behaviour. It is neither of these things. This book is, therefore, my attempt to explain what non-attachment is, why it is important, and how to achieve it. It draws deliberately on the writings of the past in order to show the subject's 'universal truth'. Its universality is only really asserted, however, because all the writings to which I refer are those of the West. Writers of the East have long accepted the idea of non-attachment. Even so, I have made no attempt to investigate Eastern writings because they operate within a different paradigm than that which operates in the West. Any attempt to do so would require, then, a particular type of knowledge and an understanding of a particular society which I do not possess and which it would be unfair to assume the reader possesses.

Ronald Shone
April 1991

# Acknowledgements

This book has been enhanced by drawings which, in large part, have been taken from clip-art provided with CorelDRAW, or drawn within CorelDRAW. I wish to acknowledge thanks both to them and the original vendors who provided the clip-art. The drawing of Mount Carmel that opens Chapter 6 is a reconstruction of St John's original sketch and is based on that found in *The Collected Works of St John of the Cross*, (see below). I also wish to thank the following publishers for permission to use selections of their material:

Penguin Books Ltd: *The Cloud of Unknowing and Other Works*, translated and with an introduction by Clifton Wolters.

For text from *The Collected Works of St John of the Cross*, translated by Kieran Kavanaugh and Otilio Rodriguez © 1979 by Washington Province of Discalced Carmelites. ICS Publications, 2131 Lincoln Road, N.E., Washington, D.C. 20002, U.S.A.

For text from *The Collected Works of St Teresa of Avila Volume Two*, translated by Otilio Rodriguez and Kieran Kavanaugh © 1980 by Washington Province of Discalced Carmelites. ICS Publications, 2131 Lincoln Road, N.E., Washington, D.C. 20002, U.S.A.

HarperCollins*Publishers*: *The Imitation of Christ*, written by Thomas à Kempis and translated by Betty I. Knott.

This book has also benefited from the assistance of a number of people. In the first instance are those individuals who wrote the great works to which this book refers. Although none of them are alive today, we can only be grateful that they expressed their insights in the printed word. The second group of individuals are those who have read parts or the whole of the book while it was still a work in progress. I would like to thank Sally Caird and Tony Phelan, and I would most especially like to thank my wife, Anne Thomson. Not only did she read the whole manuscript and make copious corrections to my English, but she also made me clarify a number of sections. Most of all, however, she has had to tolerate my attempts to practise non-attachment.

# Introduction

The most difficult thing about non-attachment is explaining exactly what it means. Only when the meaning is explained is it possible to say why it is so important. The concept of non-attachment is not alien to Western thought, it is only alien to *modern* Western thought. As I shall try to show, non-attachment has remained a central concept through all religions and throughout all time.

I begin this investigation by trying to explain the meaning of non-attachment and why it is important, but it must be realized that a full understanding of the concept will be obtained only from reading the whole book. The reason for this is that the concept can only be described in parts, and only when you, the reader, put these parts together can a full understanding of it be obtained. There is a famous Sufi story concerning blind villagers and an elephant.[1] The story goes as follows. There was a city whose inhabitants were all blind. One day the king arrived with his entourage and camped outside of the city. The king had a huge elephant which he used in battle and as a symbol of his authority. The villagers were keen to know about the elephant and some went running out to the encampment to seek it, even though they had no idea what they were hoping to find. When this group came on the elephant they began to feel a part of it, each of them exploring a different part. Each then considered that he

had knowledge of what the elephant was. When they returned to the village their fellow inhabitants were eager to hear exactly what an elephant was. From those feeling it they heard: 'It is a large, rough, thing, wide and broad, like a rug' (this from the one who had felt its ear). 'It is like a straight and hollow pipe, awful and destructive' (from the one who had felt its trunk). 'It is mighty and firm, like a pillar' (from the one who had felt its feet and legs).

Of course, each had felt only one part and had no true picture of the whole. So too with non-attachment. But unlike these villagers, we cannot touch nor hear non-attachment, nor can we see it. This does not prevent us from understanding such an abstract concept, however. We can do this by behaving in such a way that our ego is reduced. In doing this a person will come to realize something is different within him- or herself. In other words, the deliberate change in behaviour must elicit a change in subjective feeling and attitudes. It is these changes which we shall investigate in this book.

One of the main reasons why Westerners have great difficulty with the concept of non-attachment is that essentially it implies a weakening of the ego. Schooling, and the social system, with their emphasis on competition and being successful, usually require a strengthening of the ego. Consequently, a person learns to give in to the demands of the ego. To be informed that progress in self-realization can only be achieved by reducing the ego's hold on behaviour clearly comes as a shock. It goes totally against all the notions of behaviour that one has become accustomed to. But ego-centred behaviour is neither the only behaviour nor necessarily the most appropriate one for society.

As I shall endeavour to show, the psychological basis for ego-centred behaviour is fairly new and has arisen from a conception of living that stresses success in very limited terms, and stresses competition as the means of achieving it. Co-operation, rather than competition, is an alternative approach which plays down the ego. I shall try to show that a society which is based on co-operation rather than conflict is one for which non-attachment will be a central concept. However, because this discussion is more psychological in nature I have relegated it to the Appendix (see p. 173). This in no way makes it any less important, but my intention for the main part of this book is to let thinkers of the past reveal the importance of non-attachment in their own words.

In the first chapter we investigate the meaning and importance of non-attachment. We also consider different types of awareness and the meaning and importance of mortification. But agreeing upon what non-attachment is and why it is important is only a first step – although of course the first step is always the most difficult. The next step is to consider how to achieve non-attachment. It is here that we turn to the writers, religious and otherwise, of the past. Contained in these writings are methods for achieving non-attachment. The great difficulty is translating these methods into a form understandable by people today; and in a manner that can be practised in a modern society. Furthermore, I wish to make the point that such methods are not particular to any one religion, nor do they imply a religious vocation. They are a means of achieving a co-operative relationship with other people, the environment and, if you so wish, with your god.

Jung's research into self-realization and symbols[2] is useful to consider at this point. Jung was very aware that a person can come to self-realization only within a set of symbols, within a myth – a religious myth or some other myth. A Buddhist requires the Buddhist myth and the Christian the Christian myth. Each myth allows for psychic growth and a path to the truths that lie at the depths of the unconscious. William Johnston, in his *The Mirror Mind*, adds two corollaries to this Jungian view[3]: first, that anyone who wishes to embark on the search for self-realization needs faith; and second, that it is not possible to come to self-realization by one's own efforts. Christ put forward the same idea when he said that a person could only reach God through him[4].

I am the way; I am the truth and I am life; no one comes to the Father except by me.

John 14:6

If a myth such as this is true, then it is not a question of

Western man accepting Buddhism or any other myth, but rather accepting that to which each person is born. Having said this does not mean that we cannot learn from other practices. The techniques may be universal; it is only the context in which they are performed (the myth) that is different. The same point is made by Nevill Drury[5]. He argues that many investigators into 'inner space' have found that they have images that belong to the archetypes of the society into which they were born. These archetypes belong to the belief systems with which the individual becomes inculcated. Thus, the archetypes met by Don Juan, a Yaui Indian of Mexico, are different from those of a Hindu or a Christian. There is, therefore, no need to go to Mexico or the ashrams of India. We have in the West our own sources which can more readily be understood by Westerners because of our common belief systems. Even so, the message in all cases is the same: *individuals must attain loss of ego, this can be achieved only by their own efforts, and this can be achieved through non-attachment*.

It must be stressed, however:

**non-attachment is not for everyone.**

To achieve non-attachment requires such a major change in thinking and behaviour that some people may find their lives intolerable. For them the road to self-realization must take a different route. For others, it is their *present* situation that is intolerable, and they feel that they must change. Many individuals feel that a society of wars, conflict and highly competitive behaviour is one which cannot progress. It is for people of this viewpoint that non-attachment offers a means of changing themselves and society to a more co-operative basis. The road is not an easy one to travel, but to remain where you are can only mean continued dissatisfaction with yourself and with society. As St John of the Cross says within the drawing for his work, *The Ascent of Mount Carmel*[6],

To come to the knowledge you have not
you must go by a way in which you know not.

The aim of this book, then, is to outline the meaning and importance of non-attachment in order to come to an understanding of the path that must be followed if non-attachment is to be achieved. There are two elements to this: first, to give a reason for considering a new path; and second, to give some guidance on how to tread this new path. However, before we do this we need to clarify the two conceptions of god which run throughout the text.

## TWO CONCEPTIONS OF GOD

Although this book is not strictly a religious text it does, none the less, refer to 'god' throughout. This word contains within it two different conceptions, and it will be useful for the reader to distinguish between them. In Chapters 1 and 2 the predominant view is that god is a personal god, and that god is within everyone. Chapters 3 through 6 contain the Christian view of god, as expressed by European medieval writers and the Christian saints. Each conception of god implies a particular morality, and the two may not be altogether consistent with one another. It will be useful, therefore, if we clarify these two conceptions.

A personal view of god is knowledge of god which comes from within the individual. You can know individuals by their name, their occupation, characteristics, etc. But you can also know them at a deeper level if you have had dealings with them over a period of time.

You know how they think and how they react. Therefore words become a less important part of the social interaction between you. Analogously there are two ways of knowing god. The first way is that conveyed by the theologian, and constitutes an interpretation of god as separate from and independent of the individual. This conception of god is one that speaks of a reality 'out there', where god is known objectively. The second, more personal way is at the deeper level where words are less meaningful: it is a knowledge of faith. For the present let us consider further the theological view of god, and then turn to the personal view.

## A Theological View of God: the God Without

The theological view of god is that god is a being who has sole sovereignty over nature and humanity since he is creator of both. God has the attributes of being omnipotent, omniscient, omnipresent and eternal. In other words, god is in ultimate control over all things and all people; he is all-knowing; he is everywhere – although not in a spatial sense but in the sense that he is everywhere able to help and to help at all times; which gives us the final attribute, that his help is available to eternity. This conception of god differs from the personal view since god is considered to be independent of the individual: he is a god who is 'out there'. As the creator and sovereign, god is moral perfection.

Although the theological view of god has changed throughout history, the previous paragraph expresses the core idea of the theological view of god. It encapsulates the view that underlies the writings of the medieval scholars and mystics whom we shall consider later in this book.

## A Personal God: the God Within

The personal view of god expressed in the first two chapters of this book can be summed up in the phrase: 'To know thyself is to know God', a view certainly not shared by everyone. In this context a knowledge of your true self is a knowledge of god. Put another way, individuals come to know god by coming to a proper understanding of themselves. In order to come to a proper understanding of themselves they must achieve non-attachment, because only by achieving non-attachment can they subjugate their ego and develop their essence (their true self). In the Gurdjieffian system, which we discuss in Chapter 2, non-attachment (or what in his system is referred to as *non-identifying*) has to be achieved through a process of self-observation. What is the purpose of this self-observation? It is to make the personality passive and allow essence to grow. In the early part of the present book this is the interpretation we give to the phrase to 'enter the kingdom of God'. To 'enter the kingdom of God' a man must die and be reborn. This is allegorical. It is personality which must die, which must be made passive. Once this is accomplished then essence can grow, a person can 'enter the kingdom of God'. It is clear that here the 'kingdom of God' is within the individual. Spiritual development is seen as a process of reducing the hold of the ego, of constraining false personality and allowing essence to become dominant.

## THE PLAN OF THIS BOOK

After discussing the meaning and importance of non-attachment in Chapter 1, Part I of this book consists of a twentieth-century discussion of non-attachment. This is made up of Chapter 2, which discusses the work of Gurdjieff. Although Parts II and III use quotations from specific books, this is not the case when discussing Gurdjieff. Gurdjieff himself wrote little[7], and the views here are largely taken from the three-volume work by Maurice Nicoll and the writings of Ouspensky[8]. The reasons for including the views of Gurdjieff are many. First, his system has much to say about non-attachment, especially on how to achieve it. Second, Gurdjieff's system is a blend of East and West. It therefore illustrates how views that are common in the East can be absorbed and integrated into a Western lifestyle. Third, his views, at least on non-attachment, are similar to those of the medieval mystics, which demonstrates their universality. Fourth, this system gives a modern interpretation of non-attachment which is outside the Christian tradition, where it has to date largely been discussed.

It is this Christian tradition to which Parts II and III are addressed. Non-attachment has strong support in the Bible and in the works of a number of medieval mystics. In this book we shall be concerned primarily with the medieval mystics, starting from two early works: the anonymous *The Cloud of Unknowing* (written *c.*1370), considered in Chapter 3, and Thomas à Kempis' *The Imitation of Christ* (written *c.*1471), studied in Chapter 4. Although these works do not contain the depth of discussion on non-attachment that we find in the Spanish mystics of later medieval Europe, they do none the less contain some interesting observations on the subject, and highlight the methods and importance of contemplation. Although our concern is not directly with meditation and contemplation, it will be shown that the path to these is through non-attachment.

The fact that non-attachment is a preliminary step towards meditation and contemplation does not mean that once non-attachment is attained the only path to follow is towards these disciplines; far from it. One of the essential purposes in writing this book is to point out that non-attachment is the first step along many paths, of which only one is in the direction of meditation and contemplation. In the time of medieval Europe, with the wave of religious enthusiasm and mysticism, it was 'natural' to see non-attachment as the means of choosing this way. But today this direction is not the most obvious one to follow. I have tried to illustrate that even alternative routes must still take the first step of non-attachment[9]. Therefore, anything that we can elicit from these early writings will help us to understand fully what this first step entails – and even whether or not we wish to take it!

In Part III we turn to two Spanish mystics of the late medieval period: St Teresa of Avila (1515–1582) and St John of the Cross (1542–1591). It is not surprising that both of these Spanish saints were also mystics. In Chapter 5 we consider St Teresa of Avila, and contemplate to what extent she considered non-attachment in two of her works: *The Way of Perfection*, and her most famous work, *The Interior Castle*. In Chapter 6 we consider two works of St John of the Cross: *The Ascent of Mount Carmel* and *The Dark Night of the Soul*. We will find that these two Spanish mystics say far more on non-attachment than we found in the works discussed in Chapters 3 and 4. However, like the earlier works these too are intended for individuals of a religious vocation. But this should not detract from our realizing the important truths contained in them and the fact that they can apply to situations of everyday life.

What we can observe as we move through these four chapters, which are in approximate chronological order, is a growing realization of the importance of non-attachment as the first step on the road to a more spiritual life. It culminates in the writings of St John of the Cross who, as we shall see, discusses this concept the most, with a deep understanding of its significance.

Each of the three parts of the book opens with a commentary which places the individuals and their work in historical context. Furthermore, each chapter provides either a brief biography of the individual or something about the work itself. Part I opens with a commentary on the dissatisfaction that many feel in the twentieth century and their search for some form of enlightenment. A searcher of major significance, and one who attempts to blend East and West, is Gurdjieff. A brief biography of Gurdjieff is provided in Chapter 2, along with a discussion of his system[10].

A final chapter, Chapter 7, brings together some of the lessons and exercises that have come to light as a result of the study of Gurdjieff and the medieval mystics. I have decided to divide these into two: lessons first and exercises second. The lessons (there are 86 in all) that can be learned from the earlier writers are simply a summary of what we have been able to ascertain from these thinkers. Thus, their ideas are pulled together in one place. However, we have 'translated' these lessons into modern language. These lessons are followed by a series of exercises (14 in all) which will help you, if you so wish, in achieving non-attachment. In large part these exercises too have been derived from the thinkers of the past, but I have attempted to put them in terms of twentieth-century terminology, and assume that for the most part they are being practised by the average person who wishes to take the first step along the path to self-realization. There is no presumption of any religious vocation – although this is by no means precluded.

The book concludes with an Appendix, providing a psychological commentary on non-attachment. Its main emphasis is to illustrate how the development of psychology has stressed the development of the personality, while the path to self-realization stresses the subjugation of the personality. This should not be taken to mean that development of the personality is unimportant; far from it. Full development appears to require *first* a development of the personality and *then* its subjugation. Only by subjugating the ego can the next stage of development take place [11].

## End Notes

1. This story is taken from Idries Shah, *Tales of the Dervishes*, (Jonathan Cape, 1967).
2. C.G. Jung, *Man and His Symbols*, (Pan Books, 1978).
3. William Johnston, *The Mirror Mind*, (Fount Paperbacks, 1983).
4. All quotations from the Bible are taken from the *New English Bible*, (Oxford University Press, 1970), unless otherwise stated.
5. Nevill Drury, *Don Juan, Mescalito and Modern Magic*, (Arkana, 1985).
6. *The Collected Works of St John of the Cross*, translated by Kieran Kavanaugh and Otilio Rodriguez © 1979 by Washington Province of Discalced Carmelites. ICS Publications, 2131 Lincoln Road, N.E., Washington, D.C. 20002, U.S.A., p. 103. See also the illustration that opens Chapter 6 of this book.
7. He wrote only three basic works: *Beelzebub's Tales to His Grandson*, (Routledge & Kegan Paul, 1950), *Meetings with Remarkable Men*, (Picador, 1978), and *Life Is Real Only Then, When 'I Am'*, (Routledge & Kegan Paul, 1981).
8. Maurice Nicoll, *Psychological Commentaries on the Teachings of G.I. Gurdjieff and P.D. Ouspensky*, (3 vols; Watkins, 1952).

Ouspensky's main works after his meeting with Gurdjieff were *In Search of the Miraculous*, (Routledge & Kegan Paul, 1950), *The Psychology of Man's Possible Evolution*, (Arkana, 1991), and *The Fourth Way*, (Routledge & Kegan Paul, 1957).

9. In order to see that religion is but one path you only need to consider that meditation (in whatever form) provides an alternative path. Both, however, require the attainment of non-attachment in order to be successful.

10. Additional comments on essence and personality, as used in the Gurdjieffian system, can be found in the Appendix.

11. See P.D. Ouspensky, *The Psychology of Man's Possible Evolution*, (Arkana, 1991). Also see the Appendix to this book.

# 1

## Meaning and Importance

'Non-attachment', as a word, is rather unfortunate in its usage because it tends to be misinterpreted. It is useful to begin, then, with an attempt to say what non-attachment is *not*.

## Non-attachment is *not* detachment.

To detach yourself from something or someone is to isolate yourself from that object or person. To achieve such isolation is to withdraw from life; to cut yourself off from life. A non-attached person is intended to live life to the full, to be part of life in all its different aspects – physical, emotional and spiritual.

## Non-attachment does *not* mean being unconcerned about things.

Non-attachment does not mean being unconcerned about things, whether they are objects, persons or situations. This is by far the most common misunderstanding about non-attachment. To be unconcerned about things is to treat those things indifferently. To be indifferent to an apple or an orange is to treat them as equally important or unimportant. You can be indifferent to things but still be attached to them. Your indifference then only means that you treat each possibility as equally preferable, and so your choice between them is rendered immaterial. To be unconcerned about doing something is to treat that act as no more important than doing nothing. I am not suggesting that people are not at times unconcerned about things, what I am saying is that this is *not* what is meant by non-attachment. Non-attachment, then, is a certain kind of separation of the self from a person or thing. It is neither coldness nor is it a desire to shut oneself off from life.

## Non-attachment does *not* mean being unresponsive or cold.

A person may not respond to situations or to people. When a person is unresponsive to other people's feelings and actions, he or she is commonly considered to be 'cold'. The idea of being 'cold' is to have no feeling – just as in the physical sense that coldness leads to numbness and to a loss of feeling. Non-attachment does not mean to be unresponsive and cold. A non-attached person is responsive to other people's feelings and actions and is considerate towards them.

To emphasize these points, non-attachment does not mean that a person isolates him- or herself from others and society; it does not mean that such a person is unconcerned about things, people and situations; and, finally, it does not mean that such a person is cold and unresponsive.

In order to come to an understanding of non-attachment we shall approach it from a discussion of the meaning of attachment. It is slightly easier to discuss attachment and then to argue that non-attachment is its opposite. This is very much like defining relaxation as the absence of tension. So non-attachment is the absence of attachment.

## ATTACHMENT

The comparison of non-attachment with relaxation is a useful one to pursue. To say that relaxation is the absence of tension is to imply that relaxation is the act of 'letting go', of refraining from being tense[1]. The point is that you cannot *try* to relax! Trying implies effort, and effort involves tension somewhere in the body. Consequently, to relax is to stop being tense. You do not achieve relaxation by doing something, you achieve it by *not* doing something. What I shall try to show in this and other chapters is that non-attachment is also achieved by *not* doing something, rather than by doing something. Non-attachment, then, is the absence of attachment.

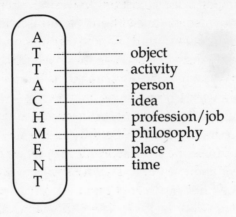

*Figure 1*  Types of Attachment

Of course, this requires us now to discuss in some detail what we mean by 'attachment'. It would be circuitous and empty at this point in the discussion to say that attachment is the opposite of non-attachment.

Attachment to something – an object, an activity, a person, an idea, a profession, a philosophy, a place or some period of time – means that you are subservient to that object, activity, person, idea, profession, philosophy, place or period of time. Your behaviour is not unconditional but rather conditional on the thing to which you are attached; that is, the thing to which you are attached governs your behaviour and responses. It is as if you and the thing to which you are attached are joined by a thread: *an emotional bond*. Accordingly, you become dominated by everything to which your self becomes attached, with which your self becomes identified[2]. Only by *misidentifying*, by achieving non-attachment, can you become in control.

We note, therefore, that attachment means having slavish feelings towards an object, an activity, a person or whatever. This is not to be confused with having a sense of love, sympathy or affection towards a person. It is possible to love someone without having slavish feelings towards him or her; and so too with sympathy and affection. It is the slavish feelings that create the emotional bond and the form that attachment actually takes. Nor must it be thought that attachment can only be to another person. One can be a slave to the accumulation of riches, to an idea, or to any one of those things denoted in Figure 1. It will, therefore, be worth considering each one in turn.

Many people have their favourite object which they cherish, which they would not part with and to which they give pride of place in their lives. In other words, they attach themselves to the object. What is more important is that the attachment is *from the person to the object*. The person chooses to become attached to the object. It is not possible for the object to choose to attach itself to a person. This means that people become slaves to the object of their attachment.

Some people may think this is not so. But consider some favourite object which you possess. Now consider how you would feel if it was taken away, broken, stolen or whatever. An attached person mourns the loss or damage of the object of his or her attachment. The attachment served some purpose (why else would you attach yourself to it?!) and this purpose is no longer being served. This is why you mourn the object's loss or damage.

Modern society places many activities in our path to which we can become attached. One of the most obvious is that of watching television, especially a favourite television programme. One of the very objectives of television is to attract audiences to particular programmes, especially to the so-called 'soap operas'. Of course, many people say that they watch these out of curiosity, or because there is nothing else to do. But how often do individuals make decisions about what to do, or what not to do, in order that they do not miss a particular episode of their favourite programme? They will rearrange meetings, eat their meals quickly, make telephone calls beforehand so that incoming calls will not be made while they are watching their favourite programme. The list of things people will do in order not to miss their favourite programme on television is endless. At the same time, however, it is quite possible to hear them in conversation saying that they are 'not bound' by television!

Although here I have concentrated on the activity of watching television, this is by no means the only activity to which one can become attached[3]. It could be playing cards, computer hacking, or simply reading a book. Whatever the activity, it is possible for an individual to become attached to it.

A more complex attachment is that experienced towards another person. A person can relate to another person on many levels and in many ways; but only one will denote attachment. However, the attachment can be *combined* with other forms of relation. You can love or hate another person, you can be sympathetic or unsympathetic towards him or her; you can show affection towards another person or show no affection; you can enjoy another person's company or not; and so on. All these feelings indicate how you relate to that person. In their 'pure' form they involve no slavish attachment. But these feelings can be *combined* with a slavish attachment – they can become 'impure'. Your love, sympathy, affection, joy, etc., can become sullied, tarnished, and even misdirected.

One of the most common forms of love combined with attachment can be seen in a person's love of his or her parents. To suggest that a person is attached to his or her parents is to suggest that he or she is a slave to them. When a parent demands a show of love and receives it then the child is combining love with slavish attachment. He or she is allowing him- or herself to become subservient to the parent's demand for a demonstration of love. (The same can also be true between two lovers.) Love needs no demonstration of proof because it will be expressed freely and readily. I am not saying, then, that a person should not love his or her parents. What I am saying is that such love can be tarnished if it is combined with attachment. The same holds true for the love between husband and wife, or between any two people. When Jesus said,

> No man is worthy of me who cares more for father or mother than for me.
>
> Matt. 10:37

he indicated that a love which is combined with attachment cannot be a true or complete love. A love of one's parents which is combined with attachment means that that person cannot freely and unconditionally love someone else – and most especially cannot freely love god.

The bond which attachment can form can be seen with respect to attachment to an idea. When you become attached to an idea then you see everything in terms of that idea. It dominates your way of thinking and binds you to it, so preventing you from seeing things in a different way. I am not suggesting for one moment that you should not have ideas. The point being made is that you may become attached to the idea to such an extent that you close your mind to different or opposing ideas. When this happens you become a slave to the idea. Nor does it matter what the idea is. You can be a slave to communism just as equally as you can be a slave to democracy; you can be a slave to monetarism just as you can be a slave to neo-Keynesianism; you can be a slave to classical physics just as you can be a slave to quantum physics; and you can be a slave to Freudian theories just as you can be a slave to Jungian ones.

A common form of attachment is to a profession or job – we have all heard the expression 'married to one's work'. People were not born simply to work. Work is only a part of living; it is a means of earning income to purchase all the goods and services a person may require. Attachment to a job arises when people consider themselves indispensable, or when they turn to work for comfort or solitude. They are then slaves to their job. They are at the dictates of the firm and the situation, just as slaves are at the dictates of their masters. This is of course to some extent a matter of degree. Anyone who works is in one sense at the dictates of the job, because most jobs usually involve specific hours, a definite work-place, and so on. The difference comes when a person becomes so attached to the job that everything else takes second place. When this happens such a person has great difficulty coping with unemployment or early retirement, since the very thing to which he or she was so strongly attached no longer exists.

Attachment to a particular philosophy is very much the same as attachment to an idea. The major difference is that a philosophy encompasses a number of ideas and the attachment binds not only the person to the philosophy but also the ideas to one another.

Some people become attached to a place: a town or city, a country, a region, or even a street or house. Like all the attachments that we have so far discussed, this too binds a person. Why a person should choose to remain attached to one place is a psychological issue, which we shall deal with later. From the point of view of our present discussion it renders such a person blind to the advantages of other places and to the disadvantages of the place to which he or she is attached. Furthermore, if for some reason he or she cannot be in that place, he or she will suffer from misery and anxiety. This is because the attachment still exists but is not being satisfied.

Finally, a person can be attached to a particular time of life: childhood, school days, teenage years, the time spent as a single person, or spent in the armed forces, and so on. But to do so means to live in the past. A person who is attached to a point in time frequently thinks about that period. This means that little or no time is left to think about the present. Attachment to an unknown future has similar problems: it too prevents a person from living in the present.

## NON-ATTACHMENT

Non-attachment, therefore, implies the absence of any slavish connection with an object, an activity, a person, an idea, a job, a philosophy, a place, or a time. The fact that we have named all the types of attachment listed in Figure 1 (see p. 26) is to indicate that there are *degrees* of attachment (and hence non-attachment). A person may be non-attached in terms of some things and not others. For instance, you may have no attachment to objects, activities, job, place, or time, but be attached to another person or to an idea or philosophy. Furthermore, an individual has a dynamic existence, which changes over time. Non-attachment may be achieved but it can also be lost. To refrain from slavish involvement in things is not easy to accomplish. We shall discuss why it is so difficult later, when we turn to explore the psychological aspects of attachment and the exercises for achieving non-attachment. The point I wish to emphasize here is that non-attachment is the absence of slavish connections, and that to become non-attached a person must learn not to enslave him- or herself.

To state that non-attachment is the absence of a slavish connection with a thing would lead people to argue that no one wishes to become a slave in this or any other sense. But this is not the case. The examples we have just discussed are very common in many societies. People *do* cherish objects; they do carry out activities at the expense of other things; they slavishly attach themselves to other people (especially their parents); they do attach themselves to some ideas at the exclusion of others; they do make themselves inordinately dependent on their job; they do attach themselves to a particular philosophy, and to certain places; and they do live in the past or the future. What we have to explain is *why* they so willingly let themselves become so attached. Put another way: *Are there any benefits to be had from being so attached?*

As we shall try to demonstrate (see the Appendix), the perceived benefits of attachment are associated with the type of society that has developed over the last few hundred years. The emotional bond that forms the attachment has to do with a psychological feature of our society, which prizes things that bolster the ego at the expense of the true self. It is because attachment is at the core of the way our society functions that we often cannot see that it is present. It is like air, which you often do not consider present – but certainly know when it is absent. It is as if society is attached to the idea of attachment!

Before we consider these much broader aspects of non-attachment it is worth considering here its importance, although a full appreciation of its significance will only be possible after we have discussed these broader aspects. Put simply: *'Why is non-attachment important?'*

Non-attachment, rather than detaching you from life, lets you live life to the full. It does this in a number of ways. First, because you are not attached to the past or the future then you live in the present. A person who lives in the past (or in the future) rarely sees, or fully responds to, the present. It is as though time moves forward but that person remains in the past. To live life to the full you must live in the present, and each present. You will then be satisfied with what you are doing, and as time moves on you will not look back only to feel that 'life has passed you by'.

Second, non-attachment allows you to see others and things as they are. An attached person becomes blind to the faults of the person they are attached to, and becomes subservient to the other person's needs, wishes and whims. When people are non-attached they can respond appropriately to others without losing their own identity in the process. They can love, sympathize and show affection to others without expecting anything in return. They give freely and without commitment. As a consequence, non-attached people can relate to others in a more meaningful and fulfilling way and without any dependence. Similarly, a non-attached person has a clear and focused mind and so can see things in their true light. In fact, this is the essence of Zen Buddhism, in which one of the aims is to possess the 'mirror mind'. The analogy is a useful one. A clear, pure and polished mirror receives all images into itself without distortion. Furthermore, it reflects all objects and images in such a way that for the objects and images it appears as if they were seeing themselves for the first time: 'so the enlightened mind is completely receptive and filled with wonder, seeing everything as if for the first time.'[4] Using this analogy, attachment leads to a blurred mirror and to a distorted image, and so the world is not seen in its true form. The 'mirror mind' is, then, only possible if a person achieves non-attachment. But as I pointed out earlier, one does not need an Oriental myth to explain this basic point. The same imagery is found in the Bible, with Christ's statement,

> I tell you this: unless you turn round and become like children, you will never enter the kingdom of Heaven.
>
> Matt. 18:3

Jesus did not say '*be* little children', on the contrary, he said '*become* like children'. The question of interest is: In what way are we to become like children? A child's mind is largely unfettered by years of ego development, and generally does not attach itself to things in a slavish way. Each object, person or situation is new and absorbing. The child exhibits non-attachment. It is in this sense that Jesus meant people to 'become like children.'

Third, non-attachment leads to relatively less anxiety and worry – with all that these bring to a person. By living in the present you do not worry about your past or your future. You accept them and respond to them to the best that your knowledge and experience will allow. By not being attached to objects, you do not become anxious at their possible loss or damage. Of course, you will be concerned if they do indeed get lost or damaged, but this is not the same as feeling a major disappointment and even possibly anger. Furthermore, a person who is attached to a place will when away from that place feel lonely and depressed, and will wish that he or she were there. Still further, attachment to a job leads to anxiety about promotion, sales or whatever. People attached to their jobs suffer greatly when they are made redundant or have to retire. A non-attached person, on the other hand, sees a job in the proper perspective and in relation to all the other aspects of life which are important to the development of the body, mind and spirit. A job is not seen as the most important thing in life.

Fourth, non-attachment allows you to have a flexible life. It does this in two ways. First, by not being attached to objects, activities, people and places you can make new friends and acquaintances without losing the old ones. You can move from place to place, making new friends. The fact that you are not attached to your previous place means that you can see the good points in the new one (whether this be a new job or a new town). As your personality changes and develops so you can acquire new objects and discard others if you consider this appropriate. The fact that you are non-attached to objects will allow you to appreciate a new object in relation to your development at that moment and not be dependent on one cherished object which simply stunts a widening appreciation of the world in which you live. Second, non-attachment means that you are not committed to one idea or philosophy. This does not mean that you flit from one to another. You may remain with one philosophy all of your life. The point is whether you are prepared to discard it if the occasion arises. Just as a cherished object is not readily given up, so too with a cherished idea.

Fifth, non-attachment brings you closer to your true self, a point we shall discuss in some detail in the next chapter and in the Appendix. For the present I shall simply state that when people come closer to their true selves they are establishing a better relationship between themselves and the environment in which they live. They are not detaching themselves from the environment. On the contrary, they are relating to it in a more appropriate and meaningful way than if they were attached to things.

# EMOTIONAL AND INTELLECTUAL AWARENESS

So far we have tried to explain what non-attachment is and what it is not; most especially how it can be distinguished from such things as being indifferent or being unemotional. Non-attachment, however, also brings into sharp focus the difference between intellectual awareness and emotional awareness: or simply the difference between the intellect and the emotion. It is most important to realize that something can be accepted intellectually but not emotionally; or emotionally accepted but not intellectually accepted. Put differently, something can be *known* at either an intellectual level or at an emotional level, but to *understand* something requires it to be known at both the intellectual and the emotional levels.

The point is that intellectual awareness is not the same as emotional awareness. They are acquired in different ways and they affect a person in different ways. Let us first take the acquisition of intellectual and emotional awareness. To appreciate the difference it must be accepted that an individual has an emotional centre and an intellectual centre. Now by *centre* I do not mean some specific organ or area of the body to which you can point and say, 'Yes, this is the emotional centre and that there is the intellectual centre.' The intellectual centre refers to aspects of the nervous system which are involved in reasoning processes. The emotional centre, on the other hand, involves the endocrine system with its series of hormones. [5] The fact that different systems of the body are involved is important in appreciating why knowledge is acquired in two quite different ways – and also why we respond to such knowledge in two very different ways.

If we accept that intellectual awareness is processed by the nervous system while emotional awareness is processed by the endocrine system, what implications follow from this? It means that a person can be influenced in three ways:

- intellectually only,
- emotionally only, or
- both intellectually and emotionally.

To what extent a person is influenced in these three different ways depends on many factors – including the type of knowledge which is being acquired.

Consider, for example, learning that 2 + 2 = 4. This is generally a purely intellectual experience. All the input enters the nervous system and is processed there. But now consider a child of 10 years old learning about zero (which is intellectually more demanding than the concept of 2 + 2 = 4). Certainly this will influence the intellectual centre, as the child grapples to understand what the teacher is trying to explain about this elusive concept. Suddenly the child 'sees', and not only knows what zero is, but why there are negative and positive numbers! The child's face lights up and he or she is eager to expound on this new-found knowledge in relation to past knowledge. In other words, the child *understands*. Not only is the intellectual centre being influenced but so is the emotional centre – as revealed by the child's smile and excitement.

Such an influence just described is by no means unique to children. It is quite possible to discuss love and hate purely analytically, where only the intellectual centre is involved. But one can also discuss love or hate in terms of some personal experience, and then both the intellectual and emotional centres are involved. A purely intellectual discussion of love or hate, for example, will take place in the cortex of the brain. The information enters the nervous system, passes quickly to the brain and there gets processed. Describing a personal experience of love or hate is, however, quite different. The description gives rise to emotional feelings which lead to chemical and other changes in the body. The more extreme the experience, the more emotion the person is likely to create in describing it. What we observe here is two different centres of the body coming into play: the intellectual centre and the emotional centre.

It is, of course, possible to acquire knowledge at the purely emotional level. But this is less common. One example of this occurs when a person is in a temper over something. Here the acquisition of knowledge and the response to it – both of which are emotional – occur at more or less the same time. That it *is* emotional is clear to note when one tries to bring the intellect to bear on the situation. The person may say 'I know what is making me angry, it is silly to be angry . . .' but he or she continues nevertheless to be angry.

The example of anger illustrates that a person can respond to knowledge in two quite different ways: intellectually or emotionally. The example also illustrates one other important aspect. The person *first* responds emotionally and *then* intellectualizes about the response. The reason for this is that the emotional centre responds more quickly than does the intellectual centre. This is so important that it is worth repeating:

> **The emotional centre responds more quickly than does the intellectual centre.**

Once responding, the emotional centre sends a whole series of messages, via hormones, to various parts of the body[6]. A person simply then responds. The slower intellectual centre may attempt to intervene, but it is generally swamped by the hormonal changes taking place within the body.

This example also illustrates the issue of identifying. If you say 'I am angry', then you are identifying with the anger: you are letting the centre of your being become identified with the person who is angry. If, on the other hand, you say something like, 'a sense of anger is trying to invade my being', then you do not identify with the anger. You keep quite separate your being, your true self, from the emotion of anger. In the case of identifying with the anger there is just one person; in the second instance there are two people: the vigilant self and the anger. To know you are angry is still to identify with the anger. You are still just one person. To observe that you are angry you must separate the 'I' which is angry from the 'I' which observes the anger from afar. Knowing you are angry is a passive act, while observing you are angry involves acting consciously in a particular way. Observing requires attention to be directed inwards. As we shall see in later chapters, the idea of having more than one self is crucial to attaining non-attachment.

What implications can we draw from this brief discussion? First, to *understand* something it must influence *both* the intellectual and the emotional centres. Second, if a response is not to be purely emotional a person requires some means of stopping the emotional response before it begins, because once it begins it must follow its own course.

But what has all this to do with non-attachment? One of the main problems with non-attachment is that it is difficult to appreciate it at an intellectual level – and this is why we have discussed it in some detail. But it is even more difficult to appreciate it at an emotional level.

**The importance of non-attachment cannot be understood unless it is appreciated at *both* the intellectual and the emotional levels.**

It is possible to read about non-attachment and about other people's experience of non-attachment, but all this will do is supply you with intellectual information.

How can a person acquire an emotional appreciation of non-attachment? There is only one way. A person must practise non-attachment; only then will it influence that person's emotional centre. Reading and hearing about non-attachment cannot influence a person's emotional centre. Individuals must observe themselves, observe what they do, what they think and how they act. Such self-observation is not intended to be a value judgement on behaviour. On the contrary, it is simply one 'I' observing what another 'I' is doing. It is a purposeful act on the part of the individual. As Huxley points out[7], the intimate nature of matter can only be discovered by undertaking physical experiments. Similarly, it is only possible to know the intimate nature of the mind and its potential by undertaking psychological and moral experiments. Thus we see that the Christian thinkers talk of mortification, humility, meditation, and contemplation. In the Gurdjieffian system individuals must engage in 'Yes/No' conflicts. Whatever the approach taken, the situation is not one of intellectualization, but rather one of action or non-action, of observing the mind and body in a particular state of being.

Furthermore, the acquisition of non-attachment is the very act that allows a person to stop an emotional response before it begins. It is because of this that a person who practises non-attachment is 'accused' of being unemotional. Strictly speaking what should be said is that the person does not let his or her emotions rule. If a person cannot control emotion then he or she is slave to them. Non-attachment does not make a person unemotional; it stops him or her from being a slave to emotion. These are quite different things.

## THE MEANING AND IMPORTANCE OF MORTIFICATION

The common view of the works dealt with in this book, and in many others, is that union with god cannot be achieved unless there is a denial of self, a subjugation of the ego. *Mortification* is the expression of this denial of self. Mortification is not particular to Christianity, but is expressed by every saint and spiritual reformer since time began. Mortification, however, should be seen as a means to an end. It is an aid to the process of union with god; it helps break through the cloud of unknowing; it helps enter and progress through the interior castle; and it is a means of educating the individual to the demands of his or her new life[8]. It is not surprising, therefore, that non-attachment and mortification are closely associated. As Underhill says,

> The death of selfhood in its narrow individualistic sense is, then, the primary objective of mortification[9].

The new life just referred to is, of course, the spiritual life and to attain this spiritual life an individual must, in psychological terms, create new neural pathways: new connections in the brain that allow the individual to progress on the road to a spiritual life. To achieve these new neural pathways an individual must do something new, and not only new, but something *active*. For only by being active will *new* neural connections in the brain come about. In simple terms, new habits must be formed and new actions performed. All these new habits and new actions, however, must be directed at sublimating the personality: sublimating the ego. More significantly, the most usual path of brain processes is to take the route of least resistance. But to sublimate the ego, energy must *not* be allowed to take the route of least resistance, and must be *directed* to a new and more difficult way. Mortification is a positive and active manifestation of this creation of new neural pathways.

The greater and stronger the mystic (or individual), the more stormy this change of life and turning of energy from the old to the new channels. *It is a period of battle.* Yet it should not be thought that mortification is a situation of death, but rather a situation of life. Or, more accurately, it is a death from which will spring life. The stronger the death the more powerful the life which springs from it. Put another way, mortification is painful, but the pain is welcomed because it is a pre-condition of blessedness.

From this last sentence, however, it should not be assumed that the greater the pain inflicted in mortification, the greater the blessedness. This was the early view of mortification, especially the act of fasting. By fasting it was thought that a person could help achieve the forgiveness of his or her sins. Such a 'merit-gathering exercise' is certainly not the intention of mortification as suggested here. Nor was it the way Christ saw it (Matt. 6:16 – 18). Just as a show of fasting (or other form of mortification) confuses the end with the means, so mortification if taken to excess then stops being a means to an end, but becomes an end in itself. Both these cases (a show of mortification and an excess of mortification), rather than leading to non-attachment, lead to attachment to mortification, especially physical mortification. That this is so becomes apparent in some individuals' self-pride in their physical pain and their condemnation of others who fall short of their degree of mortification. Rather than moving towards god, such excess simply inflates the ego and moves the individual away from god and towards a more false self. Mortification must be carried to the point of non-attachment. Beyond this it becomes overindulgent and hence an expression of the ego, most notably of the excesses of pride and vanity; and such pride and vanity is also present where mortification is openly displayed.

The Christian mystics have been renowned for their physical mortification. However, physical mortification may not be so useful as a means of achieving union with god. Certainly it is active and creates new neural pathways, as we mentioned above. It may also be viewed as a means of achieving psychic powers. St Teresa of Avila went through the most excruciating forms of self-torture, right up to her death. To what extent these were for knowledge of god and to what extent for the attainment of 'psychic' powers there is no way of knowing. These individuals may well have held the view that it was the 'psychic' powers which gave them the union with god that they so longed for. Our present knowledge does not allow us to come to a view on this matter, and may never do so.

The mortification of the flesh in Christian thought does, of course, have its roots in Jesus' various denials, including his 40 days' fast. This view appears unquestioned:

> The Gospels are perfectly clear about the process by which, and by which alone, a man may gain the right to live in the world as though he were at home in it: he must make a total denial of selfhood, submit to a complete and absolute mortification [10].

However, Jesus undertook not only physical but also

mental (spiritual) mortification. The spiritual mystics and contemplatives attempt to come close to the mortifications undertaken by Jesus. However, in the world in which we live today there are many everyday ways in which an individual can engage in mortification without withdrawing from the world and without going through extreme and harsh bodily penances. Even St Teresa was aware that the trials of living in the world can be far greater than the trials that a secluded lifestyle can provide. Life throws up ample difficulties, trials, minor sicknesses, loss of friends, family and comforts. All these are to be endured with patience and without complaint. These self-denials should be inconspicuous, non-competitive and not injurious to health[11]. They involve:

- not eating or drinking what is considered to be unhealthy[12],
- no showy acts of would-be humility,
- control of the tongue and moods,
- behaving calmly and with quiet cheerfulness (especially when circumstances or internal moods dispose us to anxiety, gloom or even excessive elation), and,
- the moment you desire something, deprive it and seek its opposite.

Simple though these appear to be, a constant striving in trying to achieve them is by no means an easy task.

Although the saints discussed in this book, and many others not considered here, engaged in extreme forms of mortification, this is not what is being recommended here. On the contrary, the self-denials listed above are sufficient to provide new neural pathways in the brain and allow a new road to be followed. The point I wish to emphasize is that mortification within Christian teaching can be viewed from quite a different perspective, and it is this alternative point of view which is suggested in this book.

**End Notes**

1. See for example H. Benson, *The Relaxation Response*, (Fount Paperbacks, 1977) and *Beyond the Relaxation Response*, (Fount Paperbacks, 1985); also E. Jacobson, *You Must Relax*, (Unwin Paperbacks, 1980).

2. This view is forcefully expressed in R. Assagioli, *Psychosynthesis*, Turnstone Books (1975).

3. The number of activities are endless. One which has attracted attention in modern society is attachment to exercise. When living becomes subordinate to exercise, then the individual is undoubtedly attached to exercise.

4. William Johnston, *The Mirror Mind*, p. 36.

5. Hormones are chemical transmitters which are released by endocrine glands directly into the bloodstream. Being released into the bloodstream they are carried to many parts of the body, including the brain. It is now realised that a number of hormones also act as neuro-transmitters, i.e., they help transmit information from one neuron to another. It is the close relationship between hormones and neuro-transmitters that is shown by the way hormones influence behaviour through their effect on brain structures.

6. Consider becoming suddenly embarrassed about something and noting adrenalin flowing through the body leading to blushing, increased heart rate, etc. The bodily responses are extremely quick.

7. Aldous Huxley, *The Perennial Philosophy*, (Triad Grafton Books, 1985).

8. This last is expressed by Evelyn Underhill in *Mysticism* (Methuen, 15th edn., 1945), p. 218.

9. Underhill, *Mysticism*, p. 221.

10. Huxley, *The Perennial Philosophy*, p. 98.
11. Huxley, *The Perennial Philosophy*, p. 135.
12. A saying of significance here, and one attributable to
    François de Sales, is: *The spirit could not endure the body
    when overfed, but that, if underfed, the body could not
    endure the spirit.*

# I

---

*EAST MEETS WEST*

# Commentary

With the decline in Christian mysticism there was also a decline in the significance of non-attachment. Although there has been a resurgence of interest in self-knowledge, this self-knowledge has not been the same as that advocated in the contemplative writings which we shall discuss in Parts II and III. On the contrary, with the rise of psychology, and most especially with the growth and awareness of personality, there has in fact been a movement in quite the opposite direction.

In the latter part of the twentieth century, however, there has been a movement (or more correctly many movements) in search of some basic truths. And if we go back to the beginning of the twentieth century, a lone figure in search of forgotten wisdom was Gurdjieff, who travelled far and wide for over 20 years. Another searcher, who also travelled to the East, was Ouspensky. These two men met up in Moscow in 1915. This was a fortunate occurrence, because it is largely through the writings of Ouspensky that we come to understand Gurdjieff. Even so, the Gurdjieffian system is rather obscure, and like so many other schools, requires teachers trained fully in the system. What is important about the system, however, is that it is a blend of East and West.

This fusion of East and West is typical of what took place in the second half of the twentieth century. Zen, Yoga and meditation are no longer confined to the East but are now practised widely in the West. Of the many different disciplines, the one that is probably the most widely practised in the West is that of transcendental meditation (or TM), as outlined in William Johnston's book, *Silent Music* (see the Bibliography). As Johnston points out, one of the significant things about this movement is that it is not confined to the devoutly or professionally religious,

> . . . there is abroad a secular or seemingly agnostic brand of mystical meditation that disclaims affiliation with any religion and is totally devoted to the development of human potential. [1]

But as yet the synthesis between East and West is not complete.

Although a number of individuals have travelled to the East in search of some form of enlightenment, while others have remained in the West but embraced Zen or various forms of meditation, especially transcendental meditation, in large part they have remained dissatisfied. If Jung is correct in his theory that man can only come to self-realization within a set of symbols, then the symbols of the East may not be capable of being fully understood by someone born and raised in the West. This does not mean that we cannot draw from the knowledge of the East, but what it does mean is that some things need to be 'translated' into symbols of the West before they can be appreciated. But there is another reason why the dissatisfaction probably remains. What we learn from Gurdjieff and the works to be discussed in Parts II and III is that self-realization does not come from outside of oneself but rather from inside. Of course, this does not mean that a teacher is therefore dispensable; far from it. Christ himself was a teacher. What must be learnt is how to obtain knowledge about oneself. It is here that the Gurdjieffian system is particularly enlightening.

However, the path to self-realization is not an easy one. The things that one should do are sometimes so blatantly simple that their full significance is not understood. In this sense, the wisdom of the past appears to be lost. Furthermore, as the emphasis on strengthening the ego increases in society, then according to the Gurdjieffian system, this will take people away from their true selves, and the wisdom of the past will become even harder to see.

As we shall see, the medieval Christian mystics advocated the subjugation of the ego. What they did not make clear is the relationship between the personality, which grows as the individual matures, and the true self, which also must be cultivated. This is dealt with fully in the Gurdjieffian system, and it is in coming to such an understanding that non-attachment plays an important role.

Whatever synthesis between East and West that does eventually materialize, it is clearly the case that non-attachment will play an important part in it. In this endeavour we shall outline here the role played by non-attachment in the Gurdjieffian system, in the hope that we can bring non-attachment into perspective as a present-day requirement for anyone who is interested in it, and not just for contemplatives.

**End Notes**

1. William Johnston, *Silent Music*, (Fount Paperbacks, 1974), p. 18.

# 2

## The Gurdjieffian System

## Know Thyself

This chapter discusses, in part, the Gurdjieffian system. It is not possible to cover the whole system because it involves a description of man's psychology and evolution, a cosmology, a series of psychological and cosmic laws, and a 'fourth way' towards the evolutionary development of man. More is becoming known about this particular system, but it is still very elusive. We do not intend to deal with all aspects of the system; on the contrary, the aim is to deal only with those aspects which have a bearing on the issue of non-attachment. It must be stated from the very outset, however, that the concept of non-attachment is central to the whole system of Gurdjieff. Before describing the way in which non-attachment is dealt with within this system, I will first give a brief biography of Gurdjieff and outline the major features of the system.

## GURDJIEFF: A BRIEF BIOGRAPHY

George Ivanovitch Gurdjieff was born in 1877 in Alexandropol in Russia. His parents were of Greek origin. His father was an *ashokh*, i.e., a poet and narrator. His father was also a wealthy herdsman, until a plague over Asia left him and his family ruined. He then turned to carpentry, something which George also did on occasion later in life. Gurdjieff's father undoubtedly left a major influence on him, as indicated by the fact that he devoted to him a whole chapter in his book, *Meetings with Remarkable Men* (see Bibliography). In this same book we find that Gurdjieff attended first a Greek school and then a Russian municipal school. It was probably this period of financial instability which instilled in Gurdjieff a sense of the importance of always being able to earn a living by some very practical means. Even at this early age, however, Gurdjieff learnt to do things differently from other people. He constantly sought knowledge of an unusual kind.

Later his search, which lasted over 20 years, took him all over the East, as far as Tibet. He was looking for the 'old knowledge', which he was sure existed in scattered places. His journey and the people he encountered is outlined in his *Meetings with Remarkable Men*. He returned to Russia in

1913, and in the spring of 1915 met Ouspensky in Moscow – Ouspensky himself had just returned from his travels in India and the East, where he was searching for a 'school'[1]. Ouspensky became Gurdjieff's pupil, and it is in Ouspensky's writing that we find the detailed account of Gurdjieff's work.

A group was formed in 1917 and met in Essentuki, in northern Caucasus, where Gurdjieff attempted to found the Institute for the Harmonious Development of Man[2]. However, the troubles in Europe meant that the group had to move on: first to Tiflis, then on to Constantinople, Germany and finally to France. They settled in France in 1922. The group finally established a resting place when Gurdjieff was bequeathed a property, the Prieuré of Avon. In fact, Gurdjieff's public life begins with the foundation of the Prieuré, and with a public performance of sacred dances (a ballet of 'The Struggle of the Magicians') at the Théâtre des Champs Elysées in 1923. Further performances were presented in New York the following year. A few weeks after his return from New York, on the road from Paris to Fontainebleau, he was injured in a car accident[3]. It was during his painful recovery that he wrote *Beelzebub's Tales to His Grandson*, the first of three works, the other two being *Meetings with Remarkable Men* and *Life is Real Only Then, When 'I Am'*. The first of these works, itself in three volumes, is very difficult reading, and deliberately so. Gurdjieff was clearly of the opinion that if readers were going to appreciate what he had to say they needed to get out of their mechanical way of reading. Reading was to be a very active experience and not a passive one.

Gurdjieff later sold the Prieuré of Avon and abandoned the Institute. From 1933 he lived in Paris. Although the Institute had closed down, Gurdjieff still had followers and groups around him. Until 1939, he occasionally visited the United States. But throughout the Second World War

Gurdjieff remained almost a recluse in his flat in Paris. He died there in October, 1949.

## GURDJIEFF'S SYSTEM

This system is by no means simple, and we cannot do it full justice in a brief section. The central idea is that the individual is 'asleep' – the quotation marks are important. It does not mean that we are asleep in the normal sense of the word, it means we are in a mechanical state, and that we respond mechanically. We have no choice in what we do, we merely respond to outside influences.

**An individual cannot *do* anything, he or she merely responds to the influences placed upon him or her.**

Part of the reason for this is because an individual is not a single 'I', but a collection of 'I's'. There is the 'I' who goes to work, there is the 'I' who makes love, there is the 'I' who does the housework, and so on. A person shifts from one 'I' to another throughout the day[4].

The system pays particular attention to the fact that all aspects of the system can be *verified by personal observation*. Nothing is to be accepted just because someone says that it is important or part of the teaching. In the present instance, therefore, we need simply to reflect on those occasions when a person, one 'I' within the person, resolves to do something. But then something happens and the resolve goes unfulfilled. This is because another 'I' takes over. This other 'I' is not the one who made the resolve, and has no intention of carrying it out!

The concept of different 'I's' also illustrates why knowing, thinking and observing are often confused with one another[5]. First, take knowing and observing. Suppose you are angry at someone. You will almost certainly know that you are angry. But this is not the same as observing that you are angry. To observe that you are angry you must separate yourself from the 'I' that is angry, in order to observe the anger from a distance (as discussed in Chapter 1). Knowing that you are angry is a *passive* act, while observing that you are angry involves acting consciously in a particular way, i.e., observing is *active*. Observing requires attention to be directed inwards. Similarly, there is a difference between thinking and observation. You may think about yourself and what you are doing, but this is also a *passive* activity. It is simply cataloguing aspects of oneself. Observing yourself, however, is *active*, and requires attention to be directed inwards. It also requires that you are separate from the particular 'I' which is doing the thinking. In other words, when you are thinking about yourself it is as a single 'I': the person doing the thinking and the person being thought about are one and the same. But to observe means to separate the observed person from the person doing the observing. There is another consideration when distinguishing between thinking and observing. Thinking is usually an activity which reflects on past events. You think about what you did on some previous occasion. Even when some event has just happened and you think about it, it is still a previous event. Observing, on the other hand, cannot be done in hindsight. It occurs *simultaneously* with the event itself. You observe what you are doing *at the moment you are doing it*. Hence observing is not only active but it is also immediate. Thinking is passive and reflective. Thus we arrive at a central teaching of the Gurdjieffian system:

> Unless a man divides himself into two, into an observing and an observed side, he can never shift from where he is. [6]

Another feature of the system is that each individual is born with an *essence*. About this essence each person develops a *personality*. Although it is essential to develop a personality, it is also essential that at a certain stage in a person's development essence is allowed to grow (this idea is developed more fully in the Appendix).

**The way to allow essence to grow is to make personality passive.**

The great difficulty faced by the individual is how to allow the essence to grow. It is here that non-attachment comes in. To make the personality passive a person must practise non-identifying – i.e., must practise non-attachment. However, a person cannot do anything, so how can he or she make personality passive? The essential way to do this is through self-observation.

**Personality can be made passive by self-observation.**

Self-observation is central to the Gurdjieffian system – 'Know thyself' is also told repeatedly to students of the system. This is not meant to encourage self-centredness. On the contrary, the point is that in observing yourself you can at least see the mechanicalness of life. In seeing this you can also see how others respond in a mechanical way; that they too respond in a way which is beyond their control. More than this, individuals are expected to achieve the ability to *be* the other person: to put themselves in the same situation as the other person, and to think and respond as he or she would do. Only those who 'know themselves' can achieve this. As we stated above, one of the main aspects of the system is that of *non-identifying*. However, in order for a person to achieve this he or she must first of all learn not to identify with him- or herself.

That is, you must realize that you are not a single 'I' but a whole set of 'I's'.

Having established that one cannot *do*, and that one can only *observe*, how can one develop essence? In this teaching, as in many others, this is accomplished only by 'friction', i.e., by the *conscious* struggle between 'yes' and 'no'[7]. To understand this struggle it is necessary to realize (again, in terms of the system) that each individual is composed of three centres:

1. the physical centre,
2. the emotional centre, and
3. the intellectual centre.

Each centre can involve a struggle between 'yes' and 'no'. Take, for example, the physical centre. Suppose you are feeling tired and think that you would like to sit down in front of the television. It appears that one's 'natural' inclination is to be idle and to do nothing. Thus, not to sit down in front of the television and instead to do something requires a conscious effort on the part of the individual. The individual is dealing with the conflict of one 'I' saying, 'Yes, sit down in front of the television and take it easy' while another 'I' is saying, 'No, don't sit down in idleness, you are only deluding yourself that you are physically tired.' It is not too difficult to think of emotional conflicts also. It is important to realize that, in terms of emotional conflicts, many of our emotional responses have been developed from past experiences, and we respond emotionally to things not consciously but rather unconsciously. The conflict is readily experienced by trying not to do what one normally does. In other words, if you are angry in certain typical situations, try not to be angry in those same situations. In doing this the aim is not to criticize, but rather to *observe* yourself consciously doing something different. Similarly, intellect can be habitual. You can disagree with some proposition not because you have thought it out, but rather because you have habitually come to disagree with such ideas. The way to see how habitual your intellect is, of course, is to try to hold the opposite point of view.

Each of these examples illustrates the idea that for a person to develop essence he or she must become involved in 'frictions' such as these. But why are such 'frictions' so important? In this system a person requires the 'first conscious shock' in order to develop. Without this shock there can be no transformation of the self.

> **Non-identifying is what supplies this first conscious shock.**

It is worth pointing out here that this idea is by no means unique to the Gurdjieffian system. A consideration of all mystical writings will readily reveal the same basic idea. Much of Christian mystical writing deals with struggle – as in St John of the Cross's *mortification of the appetites and the denial of pleasure in all things*[8]. The struggle is no more than a means of developing essence: of subjugating personality so that it becomes passive and so allows essence to grow.

To understand further the ideas of the Gurdjieffian system it is important to realize that in this system the individual is considered to have four bodies, each of a finer matter. From the first body can grow a second body, different from the first but which interpenetrates with the first. Similarly, from the second a third can grow. This too is distinct but interpenetrates the first two. Finally, a fourth can grow out of the third. Notice that higher bodies can only grow if an earlier body has been formed. It is not possible to grow body number three without having developed body number two. The first body, the physical body, is that which we are born with. Each higher body can control all the previous ones, but these higher bodies must be cultivated in order to achieve this. If they are not cultivated (the typical situation), then a person has only the physical body. Where a person has only the physical body, all higher bodies are controlled by, or are led by, this physical body, and the physical body in turn is subject to outside influences.

This situation is illustrated in Figure 2. In the upper part of the figure we have the four bodies, which are then classified   according   to   three   different   teachings:

| Teachings | 1st body | 2nd body | 3rd body | 4th body |
|---|---|---|---|---|
| Christian | Carnal body | Natural body | Spiritual body | Divine body |
| Eastern | 'Carriage' (body) | 'Horse' (feeling, desires) | 'Driver' (mind) | 'Master' (I, consciousness, will) |
| Theosophical | Physical body | Astral body | Mental body | Causal body |

———————————————————————— >

| Automation working by external influences | Desires produced by automation | Thoughts proceeding from desires | Different and contradictory 'wills' created by desires |
|---|---|---|---|

< ————————————————————————

| Body obeying desires and emotions which are subject to intelligence | Emotional powers and desires obeying thought and intelligence | Thinking functions obeying consciousness and will | I, ego, consciousness, will |
|---|---|---|---|

*Figure 2* The Four Bodies of Man

Christian, Eastern, and Theosophical. Gurdjieff himself tended to use the Eastern classification. What matters is not the terms used to describe the four bodies, but rather that these distinctions are accepted by a number of different teachings. In the middle and lower sections of Figure 2 we have the flow of influences on the individual and on the four bodies. In the middle section we have the typical flow of influences: wherein the individual is composed of only the first body, and this body simply responds to outside influences: the person cannot *do*, but can only respond. In this instance either the higher bodies do not exist, or they too are simply responding to outside influences. The arrow reflects this flow of influence.

A fully developed individual, however, who has appropriately developed each body in turn, will have control over influences. The flow of influence is from consciousness (the fourth body) down to the first, as shown by the arrow in the lower section of the figure. In other words, a fully developed person has one single 'I', and not many 'I's'. This one single 'I' influences all the other bodies, dominating in particular the physical body. The individual, instead of acting mechanically, now acts with full consciousness[9].

For our present discussion what matters is that life influences the first body, and it responds. In other words, it is purely mechanical: the internal is governed purely by the external. Part of the aim of Gurdjieff's system is to reverse this polarity and have the direction of causation flowing from the fourth body down to the first. In so doing a person's internal workings can, to some extent, become independent of the external situation. The system talks, therefore, of creating a 'deputy-steward', who organizes the internal workings of the individual. Through 'him' the polarity is reversed.

Again this idea is not unique to the Gurdjieffian system. The Bible, if taken allegorically, implies the same idea. Christ says to Nicodemus:

'In truth, in very truth I tell you, unless a man has
been born over again he cannot see the kingdom of
God.'

'But how is it possible,' said Nicodemus, 'for a man
to be born when he is old? Can he enter his mother's
womb a second time and be born?'

Jesus answered, 'In truth I tell you, no one can enter
the kingdom of God without being born from water
and spirit. Flesh can give birth only to flesh; it is spirit
that gives birth to spirit.'

John 3:2 – 6

I have quoted this passage in full because it makes it very
clear that when Christ says that man cannot enter the
kingdom of God unless he dies and is reborn he means the
birth of a higher body, and that the birth of a higher body
can only come about by the death of a lower one. While the
death is that of personality, the rebirth is that of essence.
(Notice that it does mean *rebirth*, because essence was
there initially when the individual was born, before
personality surrounded and engulfed it.) Similarly, when
Christ said 'be as little children' (see p. 34) what he means
is to be one's true self and not to be the person created by
personality.

This feature of rebirth is important both in the
Gurdjieffian system and in the Gospels, although the
Gospels do not present the three aspects of it together or
in the correct sequence. Rebirth involves three ideas:

1. death,
2. birth, and
3. sleep.

Rebirth in esoteric teaching means to stop being
mechanical and become conscious in terms of the real 'I'.

However, in order to be reborn, individuals must first awaken – awaken to what and who they are and, equally important, who they are not. Once this is understood, then the sequence is clear: awaken, death, rebirth. We cannot be reborn until we die, and we cannot die until we awaken to what we are. The awakening is to an awareness of our mechanical nature, to die is to achieve non-attachment, while to be reborn is to allow the growth of essence. Without such a death we are asleep.

The Gurdjieffian system is supposed to be a 'fourth way'. In order to understand this fourth way, then it is necessary briefly to comment on the three generally known ways. These are:

1. the way of the fakir,
2. the way of the monk, and
3. the way of the yogi.

The way of the fakir is the way of struggle with the physical body, where the fakir tries to develop physical will and mastery over his or her physical body. It involves extreme physical mortification. The way of the monk is the way of faith. It is the religious way, which is long and hard. The way of the yogi is the way of knowledge, the way of the mind. All these ways, although quite different in many respects – most notably in respect to the centre which they develop most (physical, emotional or intellectual) – have one thing in common: they all begin with a complete change of lifestyle, a complete renunciation of all worldly things.

The fourth way, however, requires no such renunciation of ordinary life. Unfortunately the first step in the fourth way is that it must be *found*. Having found it, progress is made by *simultaneously* working on all centres: the physical, the emotional and the intellectual. It differs from the other ways in that its principal demand is that individuals understand themselves.

A man must do nothing that he does not understand, except as an experiment under the supervision and direction of his teacher. The more a man understands what he is doing, the greater will be the results of his efforts [10].

More significantly, no faith is required in the fourth way. What upsets some people about Gurdjieff's teaching is that the fourth way not only involves no faith, but is in fact *opposed* to any kind of faith. But this is often misunderstood. A person *can* have faith, but only when he or she understands it, only when he or she has come to understand its truth [11].

The Gurdjieffian system has much more to it than we have outlined here, most particularly a cosmology. But enough has been said to put the discussion of non-attachment within this system in some perspective. In addition, we can now compare the ideas of this system with those of the Christian writers that we will outline in Chapters 3 through 6. It is now possible to consider in more detail what is referred to in the Gurdjieffian system as 'non-identifying', which is precisely the same as non-attachment as defined in Chapter 1 of this book.

## NON-ATTACHMENT IN THE GURDJIEFFIAN SYSTEM

The Gurdjieffian system instructs a person to non-identify. As we pointed out in the previous section, a person cannot do, the only thing he or she can do is to observe. In self-observation he or she must learn not to identify with things. Only by non-identifying with things can he or she subjugate the personality and let essence grow: only by non-identifying can he or she break away from the mechanicalness of life.

Whenever individuals identify with something, then that something has power over them. The more they identify with it the greater the power over them. As Nicoll says,

> Whatever we identify with at once has power over us, and the more often we identify with something, the more we are slaves to it. [12]

As we shall see, this very same point is made by St John of the Cross, as well as by a number of other Christian mystics. The same message comes through. People must learn to achieve non-attachment lest they become slaves to that to which they are attached.

But Gurdjieff makes another and equally penetrating point. If a person breaks away from one particular influence, one particular attachment, then the result is (usually) to become attached to another influence. The essential work on oneself within the Gurdjieffian system is to choose the influence to which one wishes to become attached. To do this successfully, then, it is necessary to know how one is attached to particular influences. Hence, we return to the maxim 'Know thyself'.

The Gurdjieffian system, however, is a practical one. It attempts to provide a means of achieving non-identification, of achieving non-attachment. The first thing one must do is to divide oneself into two: into the *observing* side and the *observed* side. Why is this so important? Only if you divide yourself into these two sides can you observe yourself with sufficient objectivity, so that you can move yourself forward from where you are. This sounds trite, but is quite important. In order to progress, in order to transform, you must move from where you are. But how do you know where you are? Others cannot tell you where you are. They can inform you of things, but only you can tell yourself where you are. But if you consider yourself as a single 'I' you cannot do this. You cannot be another person looking objectively at yourself and establishing exactly where you are. Hence, you must first recognize that you are more than one 'I'. Once you have accomplished this you can then divide yourself into the 'observing I' and the 'observed I' [13].

Force plays an important part in the Gurdjieffian system. Force can be lost, gained or created. For instance, it is possible to lose force by negative thinking, while it is possible to gain force by working on ways to prevent negative thinking. To create force, however, requires the act of 'self-remembering'.

Non-attachment is an essential element in the prevention of loss of force. Every act of non-attachment is an essential element in the prevention of loss of force. Every act of non-attachment saves force. In these terms the necessity constantly to non-attach is obvious. Only by constantly non-attaching do you prevent a loss of force, and so this must take place throughout life [14].

Once you become an observer of yourself, you have to recognize that you are really observing many 'I's' and not just one. You then observe your attachments to different things or different people. The aim of the system is to achieve objectivity. There is no right or wrong: there is simply mechanical attachments. Everything is relative and particular to the person. Hence, if person A likes chocolate bars then he must observe himself (he must observe a particular 'I' that likes chocolate bars). At this stage there is no intention of doing anything about it other than to observe. Similarly, person B may not like chocolate bars.

She too must observe herself (observe the particular 'I' which turns down the offer of a chocolate bar). Both individuals are simply observing their mechanicalness in relation to chocolate bars. But the next stage illustrates that each person must respond in different ways in order to clearly understand the nature of his or her attachment. Individual A must *refuse* to accept a chocolate bar while individual B must allow herself to *accept* the chocolate bar. In doing this each person will engage in a yes/no conflict. More importantly, in terms of the system, the individual has *consciously* chosen to engage in this conflict. Unconscious conflicts are wasteful and not part of the development process.

We see, therefore, that there is no right or wrong. What is right for one person is wrong for another. Although we have chosen the trivial example of a chocolate bar, the principle remains the same. If one person chooses not to drink alcohol then he should go and have a drink: if another person does drink alcohol, then she should refrain from doing so. Only in this way will each person engage in a yes/no conflict. In this system there is no judgement being placed on the habit of drinking. What the system is dealing with is the mechanical nature of a person's habit – whether the habit is one of drinking or not drinking alcohol.

The same procedure applies to all three centres: the physical centre, the emotional centre and the intellectual centre. Let us take an example with regard to the emotional centre. Suppose you observe that you are a person who is shy and says very little in company. This system says that to some extent you are attached to some emotional need which creates this behaviour pattern. To observe it is one thing. But to fully understand the nature of the attachment you must do the opposite. You must engage in conversation. Of course this will lead to a conflict situation. Your natural inclination is to say 'no'. But why is this your 'natural' inclination? It is only 'natural' to you out of force of habit. If you give in to the 'no' then you are merely indicating the degree of your attachment to the emotion underlying this behaviour. The aim of the system, therefore, is to enable you to talk freely when the situation demands it and to keep silent when the situation demands it. Only a person who is non-attached to talking (or silence) can achieve this. Such a person is not a slave to talking nor to silence.

A typical intellectual habit of some people is that they always find fault in others. Of course, it is often the case that such individuals never see fault in themselves. They could only find fault in themselves if they observed their different 'I's', and in particular the 'I' that keeps finding fault in others and wanting to tell them so. This particular habit is a major barrier to development. In the first instance it is merely a mechanism with which people attempt to prop up their false personality. They want to see themselves as being faultless. They can only feel faultless if they point out everyone else's faults. At the same time they are blind to their own faults. In the Gurdjieffian system the first major task is to observe yourself in the act of finding fault in others. The observation is indicating attachment, but attachment to what? It is an attachment to a false picture of yourself. The only way to break this attachment, according to the Gurdjieffian system, is consciously to stop finding fault in others, and to find fault in yourself. It should not go unnoticed that this is a basic idea of Christian teaching[15].

Whether dealing with conflicts of the physical, emotional or intellectual centre, the message is basically the same. You can only achieve non-attachment if you divide yourself into the 'observing I' and the 'observed I' and then engage in yes/no conflicts. That this is no different from Christian teaching is very well put in Thomas à Kempis's *The Imitation of Christ* (which we shall consider further in Chapter 4):

> It is the people who make an effort to overcome things they find difficult and repugnant who make more progress than the rest in virtue; a man makes progress and merits grace above all in those points where he has to overcome his own nature and die to the claims of self. [16]

In the Gurdjieffian system, therefore, life becomes a 'school'. In everything done in life you observe yourself, you decide that to which you wish to become attached, you engage in yes/no conflicts throughout. Life is a means of learning about oneself; life is a means and not an end in itself; life is a school from which to learn.

### End Notes

1. Ouspensky describes his first encounter with Gurdjieff (G, as he refers to him) in detail in *In Search of the Miraculous*, (Routledge & Kegan Paul, 1950), p. 7.
2. The Institute studied gymnastics of all kinds and exercises to develop such things as the will, memory, attention, hearing, thinking, emotion, and instinct.
3. Gurdjieff was renowned as an atrocious driver, but insisted on driving his car at high speeds. This particular accident is recorded in his book, *Life is Real Only Then, When 'I Am'*, (Routledge & Kegan Paul, 1981), p. 30.
4. This is similar to the ideas developed in Transactional Analysis, see, for example, Berne, *Games People Play*, (Penguin, 1966).
5. This paragraph is based on Nicoll, *Psychological*

*Commentaries on the Teachings of G.I. Gurdjieff and P.D. Ouspensky*, (Watkins, 1952), vol. 1, pp. 213 – 7.

6. Nicoll, vol. 1, p. 218 (original in italics).

7. Although this struggle is not the same as sin in Christian writing, it none the less states that struggle is inevitable and is to be carried out throughout one's life. Constant sin and struggle seem to be a general theme in Western thought and religion.

8. *The Collected Works of St John of the Cross*, translated by Kieran Kavanaugh and Otilio Rodriguez © 1979 by Washington Province of Discalced Carmelites. ICS Publications, 2131 Lincoln Road, N.E., Washington, D.C. 20002, U.S.A., p. 77.

9. See Ouspensky, *In Search of the Miraculous*, pp. 41 – 2; and Nicoll, vol. 1, pp. 218 – 235.

10. Ouspensky, *In Search of the Miraculous*, p. 49.

11. The fourth way is discussed in detail in the writings of Ouspensky and Nicoll.

12. Nicoll, vol. 1, p. 23.

13. This is the essence of self-hypnosis. You become simultaneously the hypnotist and the person being hypnotised. See this author's *Autohypnosis*, (Thorsons, 1982).

14. See Nicoll, vol. 2, p. 373.

15. See, for example, the quotation on p. 117 in Chapter 5.

16. Thomas à Kempis, *The Imitation of Christ*, (Fontana, 1963), Book 1, p. 79.

# II

---

## *TWO EARLY MEDIEVAL WORKS*

# Commentary

The works discussed here arose at a time when Western Europe was in the throes of the Hundred Years War (1337–1453); the Black Death was also raging, there was social unrest, and the papacy was under threat. Even in this early period there were underlying currents which would lay the foundations of the Reformation.

In Europe the best known mystic, the Blessed John Ruysbroeck (1293–1381) fused metaphysical and personal aspects of mystical truth. He was a priest in Brussels in his early years, but in his old age became a recluse in the forest of Soigues. Ruysbroeck had a tremendous influence on his own generation, and most especially on Thomas à Kempis (1380–1471) and his book, *The Imitation of Christ*.

English mysticism seems to have had its roots in the religious revival which arose during the reign of King Stephen (1135–1154), and was closely linked with the solitary life. Although there were some precursors, the English mystics begin with Richard Rolle of Hampole (*c.*1300–1349). He was followed in the second half of the fourteenth century by the unknown author of *The Cloud of Unknowing* and its companion treatises, and by Walter Hilton (died 1349), whose best known work is *The Ladder of Perfection*, both of which soon became classics of the spiritual life. Hilton's death coincides with the completion of *Revelations of Love* by the anchoress Julian of Norwich

(1343 – sometime after 1413), who was the last of the English medieval mystics. One of the characteristic features of fourteenth-century English mysticism is that it was essentially practical; it did not involve the metaphysical and speculative heights prevalent in the mysticism of other parts of Europe.

The period was one of great religious fervour. But it must be recalled that it was also the time when learning was prized and universities began to be formed throughout Europe. Information spread, partly by the movement of Christian scholars but also by books which, although written for specific individuals (often women) or orders, became quite widespread. Thus, it is fairly clear that *The Cloud of Unknowing* (1370) was known and fully absorbed by Thomas à Kempis when he wrote *The Imitation of Christ* (*c.*1471). There is even some argument that it was also known to St John of the Cross, some of whose writings are very similar. What this seems to indicate more is that the same themes were prevalent in both fourteenth-century England and sixteenth-century Spain.

In Western Christendom there is both a positive and a negative way of knowing god. The *positive* way interprets god in terms of human attributes, but god is given the highest of all possible attributes (love, light, might, majesty, etc.) Although god is beyond all human understanding, there is a continuum between man and god. God is the ultimate, and the difference is just one of quantity and not quality. This, of course, is the biblical view, that man is made in god's image and is just a reflection of god, although admittedly an imperfect one.

The alternative view, the *negative* way, is that god is unknowable, man does not know god and cannot know god, that god is qualitatively different from man. Man is dependent on god, but god is not dependent on man. All descriptions of god are thus seen as inaccurate because ultimately they are human explanations of the unknowable.

By the end of the fourteenth century, however, the general view was that god, although indescribable, was nevertheless still knowable. But how was he knowable? He was knowable through love: to know god one must love god. Furthermore, the way to approach god was through prayer. But prayer took two forms: *vocal* prayer and *mental* prayer. Vocal prayer was prayer said aloud, in words; mental prayer, on the other hand, involved silence: a devotional silence. Today the distinction made is between verbal and non-verbal prayer. In general mental prayer was considered a higher stage of spiritual development. In part this was because mental prayer was assumed synonymous with meditation, and meditation was considered the step towards learning about god.

But all this makes no sense unless it is believed that god will reveal himself to man. Belief in Christ is a belief that god revealed himself to man through Him, and will therefore reveal himself to lesser men who open themselves up to his grace. The way to open oneself up to the grace of god is through prayer and contemplation.

In achieving union with god non-attachment must be first achieved. This is recognized in *The Cloud of Unknowing*, where non-attachment is necessary in order to forge a 'cloud of forgetting' between man and all created things. It is also necessary, according to *The Imitation of Christ*, if one is to be truly 'dead of self' – and one must be 'dead of self' in order to know god. Knowledge of god or union with him is not essential. However, to know thyself, whether or not this means to know god, can only be achieved through non-attachment. Hence, the messages in the works we will discuss in Chapters 3 and 4 are of tremendous importance in our study of non-attachment and of how to achieve it.

# 3

## *The Cloud of Unknowing*

The identity of the author of *The Cloud of Unknowing* and its associated works[1] is not known, although we know from the final paragraph of the last chapter (Chapter 75), that he was undoubtedly male. Certainly from what is said in the introduction to this work the author's intention was to remain anonymous. There is little point speculating on a probable author, since no suggestion offered has been convincing. That it is a scholarly work and a work of major significance is not in any doubt. What is particularly endearing about the work is its simplicity of style, yet it reveals about its author a depth of understanding and a clear wish to know god.

There is some doubt of the date when the works were written, but the general view is that they were written in the second half of the fourteenth century, probably sometime between the appearance of the works of Richard Rolle and Walter Hilton (see p. 72). Although there are six other works generally attributable to the same author, none give us any clue as to who he was.

In order to understand the early medieval mystics it is important to realize that the general view at this time was that to know god one must love god. This is the essential theme of *The Cloud of Unknowing*. A contemplative must long to love god. In pursuit of this aim a man must become non-attached. In the *The Cloud of Unknowing* we read that

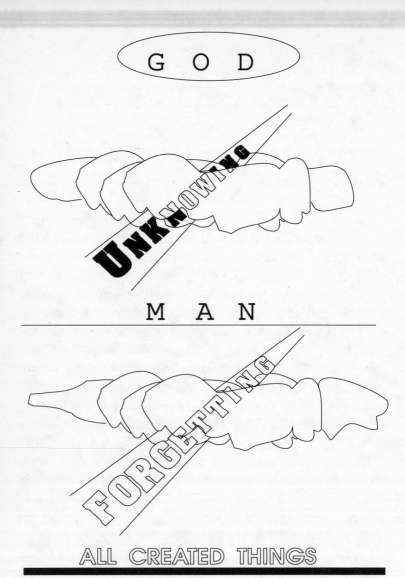

an individual must forge a cloud of forgetting between himself and all created things. There are, then, *two* clouds in this work: the cloud of unknowing, which lies between god and man; and the cloud of forgetting, which lies between man and all created things. It is in the cloud of forgetting that non-attachment plays a part.

*The Cloud of Unknowing* is a practical manual on how to become a contemplative. It points out that the demands on the contemplative are quite strenuous: a keen employment of the will, self-knowledge, humility and charity.

## THE CLOUD OF UNKNOWING

*The Cloud of Unknowing* is one of the earliest medieval works on contemplation. It is an extremely readable book, which has a simple, flowing style. Although it is largely about the path to contemplation, and breaking through the cloud of unknowing, it illustrates the beginnings of the mystic's realization of the importance of non-attachment. (In this period non-attachment was invariably referred to as detachment. As I have pointed out in Chapter 1, detachment and non-attachment are different things. However, in the writings of the medieval scholars, it was common to talk of detachment, where detachment meant precisely what I have called non-attachment.)

Although there is not a great deal explicitly about non-attachment in *The Cloud of Unknowing*, it does make a number of observations which lay the foundation for later works on the subject. It must be appreciated that when this work was written, medieval mysticism was just beginning to flourish. We shall deal with a number of these mystics – but by no means all – culminating in the Spanish mystic, St John of the Cross.

Like so many of the medieval writers, humility was essential in the pursuit of contemplation and union with god. Thus, very early in *The Cloud of Unknowing* we find the way of getting and keeping humility:

See what you still lack, not what you have already; for that is the quickest way of getting and keeping humility. [2]

We see here the beginnings of self-criticism and a constant realization of the inadequacy of self. This may seem strange in the world today, where psychiatrists and psychologists are constantly telling us that we need to 'boost our ego' and 'give ourselves positive affirmations'. However, we shall deal with this conflict, if there is a conflict, between religious statements and those of modern psychology in the Appendix.

We find an early statement of the importance of non-attachment in Chapter 3, where it is stated that in reaching god,

> Try to forget all created things that he ever made, and the purpose behind them, so that your thought and longing do not turn or reach out to them either in general or in particular. Let them go, and pay no attention to them. [3]

It is in 'trying to forget all created things' that non-attachment is being advocated. But notice that it says not only to forget all created things, but also the purpose behind them, which is a much stronger condition to be met. Only by doing this will your thought and longing not become attached to them. Even more, *pay them no attention*. This is a simple statement, but a most important one. It is the basis of much meditation. When you meditate, one of the greatest difficulties is not paying attention to many thoughts that pass through the mind. No matter how much you try to think about a single thing, which may very well be god, the mind soon goes off on its own, and within no time at all you are thinking of the shopping or something that happened during the day. As we shall see in a moment, however, *The Cloud of Unknowing* provides us with a guide for how to deal with this.

In order to understand some of the quotations we shall be presenting that offer some insight into non-attachment, it is essential to appreciate fully the basic message of *The Cloud of Unknowing*. This is set out in Chapter 4, where it says,

> By 'darkness' I mean 'a lack of knowing' – just as anything that you do not know or may have forgotten may be said to be 'dark' to you, for you cannot see it with your inward eye. For this reason it is called 'a cloud', not of the sky, of course, but 'of unknowing', a cloud of unknowing between you and your God.[4]

Thus, this cloud of unknowing which lies between you and your god is what prevents you from knowing your true self. He who knows his true self has passed through this cloud and knows god. We see here, therefore, a constant theme of medieval writing; namely, *the importance of knowing the true self*.

But having recognized that there exists a cloud of unknowing between an individual and god, then it is necessary to put a cloud of forgetting between the individual and all creation,

> . . . just as this cloud of unknowing is as it were above you, between you and God, so you must also put a cloud of forgetting beneath you and all creation.[5]

He continues to stress that he does mean everything,

> everything you think about, all the time you think about it, is 'above' you, between you and God. And you are that much farther from God if anything but God is in your mind.[6]

In other words, all the attachments you make, since these attachments are what you think about most of the time,

will take you further from your god. They do this because
they thicken the cloud between you and all creation, so
making it more difficult to break through the cloud of
unknowing between you and god.

This theme of constantly thinking about that to which
you are attached is worth discussing further, because it is
a theme which runs through much of medieval mysticism.
When you are attached to something you think about it
much of the time. Now, it is possible to be attached to
things that you like and to things that you do not like. But
the more that you like something then the more you are
attached to it, and hence the more you think about it. In
the practice of magic this phenomenon is utilized for
getting the things that you want. You think about what you
want, you behave and act as if you have it already, you
construct mental images about it. What you create in your
thoughts becomes a reality. In this particular sense, magic
*creates* an attachment while religion *breaks down*
attachments. Whether used in magic to obtain what you
want, or as a hindrance to a contemplative lifestyle, the
force of the attachment is not in dispute. Thus, in *The Cloud
of Unknowing* we have the statement,

> But if you allow houseroom to this thing that you
> naturally like or grouse about, and make no attempt
> to rebuke it, ultimately it will take root in your inmost
> being, in your will, and with the consent of your will.
> Then it is deadly sin.[7]

In magic the aim is to achieve this, but for the individual
wanting a more spiritual existence, then the aim is the
opposite and the attachment must be broken.

We pointed out above that one of the messages of *The
Cloud of Unknowing* was to pay attachments no attention,
because only by so doing can you break the attachment.

But how is this accomplished? Chapter 7 of the work provides a very simple, yet effective, means of 'right thinking'. You choose a word of one syllable, such as '*god*' or '*love*'. You then fix this word deep into your consciousness so that it is always there when you need to call on it. With this word you shield yourself from incorrect thoughts. In other words, the moment an incorrect thought enters your head you replace it with this one word. Hence it is by means of this one word that you help to dispel the cloud of unknowing. The importance of doing this is explained later in the text, in Chapter 9. If a thought can rise unbidden and take your thoughts away from god, then how much more will a thought take you from god if it is deliberately entertained because it concerns something to which you are particularly attached. The fact that attachments mean we think about these things constantly means that we cannot be thinking simultaneously about anything else, most especially god. Thus, *The Cloud of Unknowing* states,

> For if the bare thought of anything at all, rising unbidden in your mind, serves to remove you further from God than you would otherwise be (it gets in your way and renders you less able to experience his love), how much more frustrating will be the thought that is deliberately entertained and sustained?[8]

The problem that appears with attachments is that they give pleasure and delight, and because of this a person dwells on them, paying them attention at the expense of other things. Depending on what it is, *The Cloud of Unknowing* claims that the attachment is either pride, avarice, gluttony or lust. However, all this illustrates is that it is possible to classify attachments in many ways. For our purposes we shall just use the classification given in Figure 1 (see p. 26).

In Chapter 13 of *The Cloud of Unknowing*, the author returns to the topic of humility. Humility is imperfect when it arises from mixed motives. It is perfect only when it is caused by god. But the book says something more, which not only states the importance of knowing one's true self, but claims humility is nothing other than a knowledge of one's true self,

> In itself, humility is nothing else but a true knowledge and awareness of oneself as one really is. For surely whoever truly saw and felt himself as he is, would truly be humble. [9]

We see in this discussion of humility two ideas which are taken up by later writers. First, the idea of *imperfect* virtue, or mixed motives. Second, and more important from the point of view of this study, the idea that humility is nothing other than a knowledge of one's true self. Some writers go as far as stating that to know oneself is to know god. Whether this is true or not, the importance of knowing one's true self is a theme which runs through the medieval scholars and appears again in Gurdjieff – not to mention Eastern thought. Exactly what the 'true self', is and how knowledge of it can be achieved, is in large part the subject of this book.

Throughout *The Cloud of Unknowing* one finds 'exercises' to aid the contemplative. In Chapter 28 we find that before a man can become a contemplative he must cleanse his conscience, while in Chapter 32 we find two spiritual 'dodges' for achieving this:

> Do everything you can to act as if you did not know that they were so strongly pushing in between you and God. [10]

and

> When you feel that you are completely powerless to
> put these thoughts away, cower down before them
> like some cringing captive overcome in battle, and
> reckon that it is ridiculous to fight against them any
> longer. [11]

In this second 'dodge' once you become powerless you no
longer resist but, on the contrary, surrender yourself to
god. It is in this surrender that you perform an act of
humility.

In *The Cloud of Unknowing* we find the beginnings of the
idea of the importance of non-attachment. Only through
non-attachment can one create a cloud of forgetting
between oneself and all created things; and only by doing
this can one break through the cloud of unknowing
between oneself and god. Stripping away the religious
connotations, one can only know one's true self if one first
achieves non-attachment. This is not easy and must be
constantly strived for. When one finds oneself thinking
about something one is attached to, then a method of
breaking this attachment is to think of a single word or
phrase which has already been lodged deep in one's
consciousness. For this to work, however, the word or
phrase must be powerful enough to break the bonds of
attachment. In other words, it must be powerful enough to
remain in one's consciousness. By so doing it prevents the
thoughts surrounding the attachment to take hold.

## End Notes

1. These anonymous works, which appear to have been
   penned by the same individual, comprise *The Cloud of
   Unknowing*, the most famous of all, *The Epistle of Privy*

*Counsel*, which appears to have been written later in the person's life, and *Dionysius' Mystical Teaching* and *The Epistle of Prayer*.

2. *The Cloud of Unknowing and Other Works*, translated by Clifton Wolters, (Penguin, 1961), p. 60.
3. Wolters (tr.), *The Cloud of Unknowing*, p. 61.
4. Wolters (tr.), *The Cloud of Unknowing*, p. 66.
5. Wolters (tr.), *The Cloud of Unknowing*, p. 66.
6. Wolters (tr.), *The Cloud of Unknowing*, p. 67.
7. Wolters (tr.), *The Cloud of Unknowing*, p. 75.
8. Wolters (tr.), *The Cloud of Unknowing*, p. 74.
9. Wolters (tr.), *The Cloud of Unknowing*, p. 78.
10. Wolters (tr.), *The Cloud of Unknowing*, p. 98.
11. Wolters (tr.), *The Cloud of Unknowing*, p. 98.

# 4

## *The Imitation of Christ*

In Thomas à Kempis's book, *The Imitation of Christ*, there are many references to the act of non-attachment. Like a number of religious texts, there is some dispute as to the authenticity of this work, but what is not questioned is its importance in the history of Christianity. It had a major influence in the fifteenth century when it was first published, and has been influential to this day. It is a very practical book, written in a simple style, and retaining its relevance in all ages – which is one of its most remarkable features. It is generally recognized to be composed of four books, which originally were written as four separate treatises.

We begin, however, with some preliminary remarks on Thomas à Kempis and on this major work.

## THOMAS À KEMPIS

Thomas à Kempis was born *c.*1380 in Germany, 40 miles outside Cologne; he was the younger of two brothers. In 1392 Thomas was linked to the Brethren of the Common Life, whose ideals were poverty, chastity and obedience. In order to foster charity and humility the order discussed together personal spiritual problems. Thomas was particularly helped by Florentius Radewyn, rector and by then leader of the movement. There is no doubt that Thomas would have observed their practices and listened to their spiritual discussions, but it is quite clear that it was Florentius Radewyn who had the greatest impact on him.

After joining the monastery of Mount St Agnes, where his brother John was prior, he was accepted as a novice after John's departure. In 1413 he was ordained a priest. Throughout the 1430s and 1440s Thomas held a number of offices which kept him busy, but he still found time to write. These writings included works on his duties, sermons, prayers, poems and books on the monastic life. He also wrote historical texts. He died in 1471.

*The Imitation of Christ* is usually attributable to Thomas à Kempis, although there is some dispute about its authorship since it was officially an anonymous text. What is certain is the significance and popularity of the work. Written during the early years of the fifteenth century (certainly it was known by 1427), it was soon translated into many languages. It is made up of four books, which were originally written as four separate treatises[1], but they were soon put together as part of the works of Thomas à Kempis under the title *The Imitation of Christ*.

## THE IMITATION OF CHRIST

Book 1 deals with the temptations and difficulties that an individual will encounter when he or she decides on a devotional life. It was probably written for novices who intended to become part of a monastic order. The basic themes are of separating oneself from the world and from worldly wants and desires. Of course, this is the basis of all monastic practices, the purpose being that the individual can direct all his attention to god. The individual must want nothing more than knowledge of god; and to do this he must acquire self-knowledge[2]. Furthermore, he must suppress all links with the external world and in so doing curb his natural instincts, desires and emotions.

The follower of Christ must resist sin, he must be constantly watchful of his actions and his innermost thoughts. Only by self-examination can the individual realize the extent of his sin in word, deed or thought. What the individual has to come to accept, in terms of this work, is that he cannot escape sin and that he must constantly be on his guard to avoid sinning. In these terms life is a constant struggle[3]. A large part of Book 1 is devoted to recognizing the trials that a person must meet and the ways of overcoming them, which we shall deal with later.

Book 2 is more about the gains which a person can achieve if he can separate himself from the external world. If he can achieve this he attains humility[4]. Furthermore, he acquires a quietness and joy which can be preserved no matter what is happening in the external world. However, Book 2 also indicates that this can be achieved only by constant suffering. The 'suffering' does not mean physical suffering (although this may be a part of it), what it means is that the individual must constantly avoid sin. There does not come a point when a person no longer sins. Because of this the individual must constantly be on his guard. In this sense he must constantly struggle, and in the struggle must constantly suffer.

Books 3 and 4 are more about the union with god that can be achieved when the struggle is successful, when non-attachment is achieved and maintained. Book 4, which we are not concerned with here, is specifically about the Christian sacrament of Holy Communion.

The value of *The Imitation of Christ* is not in the fact that it deals with the requirements for a monastic life, but rather that these same basic principles hold if one is to follow a Christian way of living: of living a Christian life. The common sense approach of *The Imitation of Christ* can be sensed immediately. It is as if the words hit our emotional centre as well as our intellectual centre, as discussed by Gurdjieff and outlined in Chapter 1 of this book (see p. 36).

In the discussion which follows I am not assuming that the reader is about to enter into a monastic life. My intention is to discuss the underlying themes of *The Imitation of Christ* in respect to its emphasis on non-attachment. It will be clear from what has been said so far that non-attachment is a major theme within Book 1 of Kempis's original work. It is also clear that it is this which underlies the Christian approach to sin and suffering.

*Mortification of the flesh*, however, can be taken too far, as was pointed out in Chapter 1.

It must constantly be kept in mind that non-attachment means non-attachment to physical things, emotional things and intellectual things. A number of early mystics, such as St Francis of Assisi, went to extremes in their physical suffering in order to achieve non-attachment to the body.[5] But such actions are one-sided and extreme. There is nothing in the interpretation of sin and suffering that requires such extreme mortification. This was simply one interpretation, that of the medieval saints and mystics.


## THE IMITATION OF CHRIST AND NON-ATTACHMENT

As in many of the works I am discussing, there is a constant realization that each person is more than just one being[6]. The difficulty of interpreting many of these works is that of establishing how they distinguish various aspects of the individual. In *The Imitation of Christ* the author talks of 'self' and being 'dead of self'. Of course, he is not speaking of the actual person who walks and breathes. What is meant is some aspect of the *personality* which is attached to worldly things and prevents the individual from forming the only worthwhile attachment: namely, attachment to god. In trying to achieve this, Christian writing repeatedly makes the point that an individual must despise himself,

The highest and most profitable form of study is to understand man's inmost nature and despise it; real wisdom and perfection lie in having no high opinion of oneself, but in always thinking highly of others.[7]

In this quotation we also see the emphasis placed on understanding one's innermost nature: in other words, people must come to understand themselves. Only by understanding themselves can people overcome themselves. And overcoming themselves is the hardest struggle of all,

> No one has a harder struggle than the man who is striving to overcome himself. [8]

In this struggle the aim is to be 'dead of self', to achieve non-attachment; for,

> The man who is not perfectly dead of self is easily tempted; small and petty things defeat him. [9]

In Book 1 of *The Imitation of Christ* there are many references to improving oneself, to progressing. Progress, however, can only be achieved by struggle, and this struggle is no more than the attempt to achieve non-attachment. Such battles are there in order to make us victorious:

> It is a good thing that we have to face difficulties and opposition from time to time, because this brings us back to ourselves; it makes us realize that we are exiles and cannot pin our hopes on anything in this world. [10]

This rather austere view is typical of medieval Christian thought. Discipline and penitence are just some of the actions advocated:

> We can be sure of dying happily if our lives show an utter disregard of the world, a fervent desire for

progress in virtue, a love of discipline, the practice of penitence, readiness to obey, denial of self, and acceptance of any adversity for the love of Christ. [11]

It would appear, then, that *The Imitation of Christ* advocates much more than just non-attachment. It is true that denial of self is a main theme, but so are discipline, penitence and mortification. However, it could be argued that penitence and mortification are just means of achieving non-attachment.

Again, there is a message in this medieval work concerning how to achieve non-attachment: by overcoming things one finds difficult and even repugnant. It is very easy to overcome a problem about something that one is not attached to; it is much harder to overcome a problem about something that one is attached to.

> It is the people who make an effort to overcome things they find difficult and repugnant who make more progress than the rest in virtue; a man makes progress and merits grace above all in those points where he has to overcome his own nature and die to the claims of self. [12]

And again,

> Your old self needs to be put to death most of all perhaps at those times when you have to see and submit to something that you do not like, especially when you are ordered to do inconvenient things that do not seem very useful. Since you are a man under authority, it is a question of not daring to resist the power set over you, and so you find it hard to give up all right to your own opinions and live your life at another's beck and call. [13]

What is also clear from these quotations is that it is simply not struggle for its own sake which is being advocated. The person must struggle against those very things which are part of his or her own nature. In order to struggle against things in one's own nature it is first necessary to understand oneself.

Book 2 of *The Imitation of Christ* goes on to point out that the purpose of doing all this is to achieve communion with god.

> Learn indifference to all that lies outside you and devote yourself to the life within, and you will see the kingdom of God coming in you. [14]

But on a more practical level, this discipline allows individuals not to become a slave to anything and everything that is going on around them. They can to some extent control their innermost selves independently of outside circumstances.

> The man who is living the inward life can soon still all his thoughts, because he never abandons himself entirely to outward things. No physical toil is any obstacle to him, nor any activity that must be performed – he can adjust to anything that comes. [15]

That this advanced level of inward life is difficult, and that only a few can attain it, is acknowledged in Book 3:

> Only if a man is loosed from all created things is he free to direct his will to the things of God. The reason why so few contemplatives are found is that few people know how to cut themselves off completely from all that is perishable and created. To do so one needs a great grace that can raise the soul and transport it beyond itself.

Unless a man is uplifted in spirit, released from the ties of every created thing and wholly united to God, it does not matter much what he knows or possesses. He will long remain spiritually weak and unable to rise, if he thinks anything of value other than the one immeasurable, eternal Good [*sic*]. Whatever is not God is nothing, and must be considered nothing.[16]

In this next extract, however, we can see all aspects of what the individual must do in order to achieve progress.

THE VOICE OF THE LORD: My son, you cannot have complete freedom unless you deny your own claims entirely. Men are in chains as long as they have possessions and love their own interests, as long as they are covetous, curious and unsettled, always looking for what is easy and not for the way of Jesus Christ, fashioning and building something that will not last. For everything will perish that does not spring from God.

Hold on to the brief saying that sums this up – leave everything and you will find everything; abandon desire and you will discover rest. Meditate on it, and when you have put it into practice, you will understand everything.[17]

In this quotation the statements *leave everything and you will find everything; abandon desire and you will discover rest* are very similar to those of St John of the Cross, whom we shall discuss in Chapter 6.

This theme gets repeated in many forms. This should not be surprising. We have already seen that non-attachment is a form of surrender. However, it is not a once-and-for-all surrender. It must be done constantly throughout life, it must be done in small things as well as in large ones. As we have noted earlier, this is not only typical of Christian writing, it is also true of the Gurdjieffian system. But it could also be said that this is the reason why a number of Christians have undertaken mortification of the flesh for long periods of time. *The Imitation of Christ* makes the point very forcibly:

> THE VOICE OF THE LORD: My son, give up self and you will find me. Lose the right to choose and the right to own, and you will know nothing but gain. Abundant grace will be heaped upon you the moment you surrender your own will and do not claim it back again.
> THE DISCIPLE: O Lord, when shall I surrender myself? at what point give up my claims?
> THE VOICE OF THE LORD: Always and at every moment, in small things and in great. I allow no exceptions, but want to find you naked of everything. Besides, how can you be mine or I be yours, unless you are stripped of all self-will, both within and without? The sooner you do this, the better it will be for you; and if you do it with honesty and thoroughness, you will please me all the more, and gain all the more for yourself. [18]

The practical nature of *The Imitation of Christ* is very well illustrated by the advice which says that it is relatively easy to give up something that you dislike. What is much more difficult to do is to give up something that you like; alternatively, it is easy to do a job that you like doing, but it is much harder to do a job that you dislike doing.

> Your old self needs to be put to death most of all perhaps at those times when you have to see and submit to something that you do not like, especially

when you are ordered to do inconvenient things that do not seem to be very useful. [19]

It can be seen that throughout the first three books of *The Imitation of Christ* there is constant reference made to the means and benefits of non-attachment. At no time is it said that this will be easy; on the contrary, it is admitted that the struggle will be hard. This is because our nature seems to be such that we wish to take the easy route. But the easy route is simply giving in to our personality. The progress referred to in *The Imitation of Christ* is the progress of the spirit. To achieve such progress a person must achieve non-attachment. It is of course true that *The Imitation of Christ* is a Christian text, and as such the aim of non-attachment is to achieve union with god.

> THE VOICE OF THE LORD: My son, you can only enter into my being as you escape from your own. It is when you desire nothing from the world outside that inward peace will be yours; and it is when you give up self in your inmost thoughts that union with God will become a reality.
>
> It is my will for you to learn complete denial of self, accepting my will without rebellion or complaint. [20]

But non-attachment is a method of living and does not necessarily have to be associated with the achievement of union with god. It can apply equally to living life in a better and more meaningful way[21]. This greater meaning comes from self-knowledge, and self-knowledge is aided by achieving non-attachment.

**End Notes**

1. The four books are: *Counsels on the Spiritual Life, On the Inner Life, On Inward Consolation,* and *On the Blessed Sacrament.*

2. Self-knowledge, or 'Know thyself' is a theme which runs through Eastern as well as Western religious thinking. It is certainly a main tenet of the Gurdjieffian system discussed in Chapter 2 of this book.

3. This has been one of the accusations levelled against Christianity, that is, that it portrays life as a constant struggle – sin is seen as inevitable and life as a process of resisting it. Some consider this a rather negative view of life.

4. Humility is a theme which we come across throughout Western Christian teaching. As we shall note in Chapter 5, it is the main subject of St Teresa's *The Interior Castle.* Even so, it is not alien to Eastern thought, either. Consider the following koan (a *koan* being a riddle used in Zen to teach inadequacy of logical reasoning), which occurs in the Mumonkan (Case 21) and is meant to be illustrative of humility:

   A monk asked Unmon, 'What is the Buddha?' Unmon replied, 'A shit-stick' [used at this time in China instead of toilet roll].

5. St Francis exemplified the typical Christian paradox of 'joy in suffering'. Perfect freedom, thought Francis, could only be achieved by the death of 'Brother Body'. Even Thomas More, who was indeed a Renaissance man, almost certainly engaged in self-flagellation as a form of penance. Moreover, St Teresa inflicted extreme self-torture right up until the time of her death.

6. This is most especially true of the Gurdjieffian system as discussed in Chapter 2.

7. Thomas à Kempis, *The Imitation of Christ* (Fontana, 1963), Book 1, p. 39.

8. Kempis, *The Imitation of Christ*, Book 1, p. 41.
9. Kempis, *The Imitation of Christ*, Book 1, p. 45.
10. Kempis, *The Imitation of Christ*, Book 1, p. 52.
11. Kempis, *The Imitation of Christ*, Book 1, p. 73.
12. Kempis, *The Imitation of Christ*, Book 1, p. 79.
13. Kempis, *The Imitation of Christ*, Book 1, p. 188.
14. Kempis, *The Imitation of Christ*, Book 2, p. 83.
15. Kempis, *The Imitation of Christ*, Book 2, p. 85.
16. Kempis, *The Imitation of Christ*, Book 3, p. 160.
17. Kempis, *The Imitation of Christ*, Book 3, pp. 161 – 2.
18. Kempis, *The Imitation of Christ*, Book 3, pp. 168 – 9.
19. Kempis, *The Imitation of Christ*, Book 3, p. 188.
20. Kempis, *The Imitation of Christ*, Book 3, p. 203.
21. It could be argued that non-attachment is a method of relating with the unconscious mind – i.e., the right brain. Union with god, then, is possibly no more than becoming a fully integrated human being.

# III

---

*TWO SPANISH MYSTICS*

# Commentary

Medieval Spain was composed of two contrasting civilizations: one the Christian religious group and the other composed of Moslems, Arabs and Berbers. The two groups struggled for almost 500 years in order for one or the other to achieve supremacy. By 1266 most of Spain, with the exception of Granada, had been reclaimed for the Roman Church. Christian Spain was, however, far from united. The kingdoms of Portugal and Castile, of Aragon and Navarre, each went their own way, developing their own divergent interests. Even so, Christian Spain was in all respects a province of France (as was also true of its art world). In the eleventh century the Spanish religious houses obeyed the rule of Cluny, and took after the house of Cîteaux. This French influence was most true in the architecture of Spain's cathedrals and churches. The Christians finally emerged victorious when Ferdinand and Isabella conquered Granada. The way was now cleared for complete Catholic dominance of Spain.

Spain had for the most part escaped the outbreak of mystical life which had swept through Europe in the early and late middle ages. Spanish mysticism first appears in connection with the religious orders, most especially the Franciscans and Augustinians. These orders flourished although outside of the Church, and in spite of the efforts of the Inquisition. Although taking a variety of forms they shared a common purpose: to challenge the pomp and ambition of the papal see, its sacraments and ceremonies and its claim that the priesthood had special claim to divine authority. It must be emphasized, however, that these new religious orders did not take objection to the sacraments themselves, their objections were to the claim made that the sacraments conveyed 'divine grace'.

The most characteristic form of Spanish mysticism found its expression in the life and personality of St Ignatius Loyola (1491–1556), the founder of the Society of Jesus and the man whose *Spiritual Exercises* have been an inspiration to many. Originally a soldier and a visionary, he received a wound when fighting in Navarre in 1521 which left him lame for life. It was during his slow and agonizing recovery that he turned to god. He was determined to become a soldier of Christ. No mortification of the flesh was too rigorous for St Ignatius. His life and work became an inspiration to St Teresa of Avila (1515–1582) and St John of the Cross (1542–1591), the two Spanish mystics we shall be considering in the next two chapters.

The Protestant Reformation presented a major challenge to the dominance of Rome and the papacy. Had the temporal powers of sixteenth-century Europe united against the Lutherans of Germany and the Calvinists of Geneva, then they might have succeeded in preventing the spread of Protestantism. They were, however, far from united. The result was an expansion of Protestantism which was both far-reaching and fast-moving. In 1559 Henry II of France turned his attention away from Italian conquests and to the heresies at home. So began the religious wars. The religious war in France lasted, with intermissions, from 1560 until the Edict of Nantes in 1598. This Edict secured for the Protestant Huguenots the promise that their religious faith would be tolerated and that they would be given a privileged position within the French kingdom.

Both St Teresa and St John of the Cross belonged to the Carmelite Order. This Order originated in Palestine, at the foot of Mount Carmel. It was originally composed of hermits who were dedicated to a life of extreme austerity. In the thirteenth century, members of the Order migrated to all parts of Europe. However, as the Carmelite movement spread the observance of its rules were relaxed, so that by the time the Convent of the Incarnation was founded at Avila the original Rule had become very lax indeed. It was St Teresa who attempted to reform the Carmelite Order, intending to bring it closer to its original observances. Following a vision, St Teresa set on the idea of founding a convent of Discalced (i.e., barefoot) nuns who would observe the original strict form of the Carmelite Rule. After much difficulty, she founded the Convent of St Joseph at Avila. This was followed by other reformed houses, including some for men. It was at this time that St Teresa met St John of the Cross, at the time that she was arranging for a house at Duruelo to be converted for the new Order. It was John who put the house at Duruelo in order.

# 5

## *St Teresa of Avila*

St Teresa of Avila spent most of her life in an enclosed convent in sixteenth-century Spain. Having little formal education, her writings are remarkable for the impact they have had on generation after generation of students and believers. But they are more remarkable in having been written at a time when Spain was strongly anti-female, a sentiment expressed not least among theologians. In part this was because the academic theologians of her time were very much influenced by Aristotle's view of women: that they are ruled more by their emotions than by logic.

## ST TERESA OF AVILA: A BRIEF BIOGRAPHY

St Teresa of Avila (1515 – 1582) was born Teresa Sánchez de Cepeda y Ahumada. She had two sisters and seven brothers. At the age of 16 she entered a local school run by Augustinian sisters as a boarder; she stayed there for about 18 months. It was here that she was influenced by a friend from the Carmelite Convent of the Incarnation, and it was this Order which she decided she would join if she were to take her vows. She joined the convent in 1536, when she was 21. The next 20 years of her life were spent in a constant struggle between flesh and spirit. She was rarely

PERFECTION

in good health, suffering from frequent fits, heart pains and various other ailments.

It was during her first years with the convent that St Teresa was introduced to the *Third Spiritual Alphabet*, written by Francisco de Osuna, which contained instructions on mental prayer. With this book as her guide, she spent time in solitude and prayer.

The Convent of the Incarnation at Avila was based on the Carmelite Rule; however in this it was rather lax with regard to the original canon of solitude and prayer, being only a partially enclosed convent. Although critical of this, St Teresa drew comfort and inspiration from the *Confessions* of St Augustine. It was during this time that she developed the techniques which led to mystical experiences, such as envisioning Christ within herself. Having decided that she was destined for a contemplative life, she so began her second conversion, described in detail in her auto-biographical work *The Life of St Teresa* and in her work entitled *The Interior Castle*.

Within this period of contemplation St Teresa had the idea to found a convent of Discalced (barefoot) nuns who would observe the first Order of the Carmelite Rule. Thus she founded the Convent of St Joseph at Avila. She died in 1582 and was canonized in 1622, and in 1814 was proclaimed the patron saint of Spain.

## TWO IMPORTANT WORKS BY ST TERESA

In sixteenth-century Spain religion and politics were closely entwined. In the opening chapter of *The Way of Perfection* we find St Teresa discussing the problems within the Church and referring to the troubles in France, commenting (rather scathingly) on the 'havoc the Lutherans had caused and how much this miserable sect was growing.'[1] It would appear, however, that this was St Teresa's way of talking about Protestantism, albeit in a vague (not to say inaccurate) way. She was, of course, referring to the religious wars between the Catholics and the Huguenots. Catholic Spain had a strong reaction against Protestantism, which was viewed as almost akin to the plague by both civil and ecclesiastical rulers. But this reaction created a problem for St Teresa and for her superiors. Erasmus and the *Alumbrados*[2] emphasized mental prayer, the act of silence, very strongly, and down-graded vocalized prayer and all the other rituals usually associated with it. In the eyes of some theologians, within mental prayer lay the seeds of Protestantism. Some even complained to the Inquisition of the spread of mental prayer among the general population, especially among women. Already in 1559 there was published an index of forbidden books, which included almost all books dealing with prayer. In short, vocalized prayer was felt to be quite sufficient for the general population.

This then was the atmosphere in which St Teresa founded her monastery for women who would dedicate themselves to a life of prayer. In *The Way of Perfection* St Teresa stresses both vocal and mental prayer (arguing that mental prayer was not properly understood); she argues that both are an aid to perfect contemplation. It is not surprising, then, that this group of women (around 11 or 12 in number, initially) would be looked upon with suspicion. Furthermore, it is in this light that one should view the reticence of Domingo Báñez, St Teresa's confessor, in his forbidding her writings to circulate freely, especially her *Life*, which more than any other of her works deals with mystical experiences.

The group of women who came together to form the Order at St Joseph's in Avila took support from the Carmelite Rule. In the past, hermits had spent periods of time in rugged solitude and contemplation on Mount Carmel in Jerusalem. It was these hermits who became the inspiration for the Carmelite Order. A central element of this Order, therefore, was incessant prayer; and prayer requires peace and solitude.

It is against this background, then, that the writings of St Teresa of Avila should be considered. Although she wrote much, in this chapter we shall be considering only two of her better known works: *The Way of Perfection* and *The Interior Castle*. The latter is her best-known work.


## THE WAY OF PERFECTION

As we have pointed out, *The Way of Perfection* was written at the behest of the Sisters of St Joseph, who, having heard about St Teresa's *Life* and the instructions contained therein, wished her to write a book especially for them[3]. However, in this case the instructions given were to be more practical in nature than those contained in her *Life*. What the sisters requested were specific instructions on prayer and contemplation. St Teresa's writing style is clearly brought out in this work. She writes as if she were holding a conversation with her Sisters of St Joseph; and her conversational style is flowing, with many digressions – which some people find endearing and others annoying.

*The Way of Perfection* was probably written in 1566, which is also the year that the second version was most likely written. The whole book, consisting of 42 chapters, is about prayer and contemplation. Here, however, our particular interest is only in her remarks with regard to non-attachment, which occur in the earlier chapters. The central message of the book, and one which includes non-attachment, is contained in Chapter 4. Here she says that she will enlarge on three things, for it is in practising these three things that aids in the possession, both inwardly and outwardly, of the peace of the Lord. These are:

1. love for one another,
2. detachment from all created things, and
3. true humility,

of which the most important is humility, since it is humility which encompasses all the others. It is not surprising, therefore, that humility is a motif that runs through all of the writings of St Teresa.

Love for one another is important, but excessive love is destructive. Excessive love means that a person cannot love others equally. It also means desiring possessions in order that gifts can be given to the one that is excessively loved. In terms of the Order, it means turning one's attention away from the love of god. Although she turns to detachment later, what we observe here is its opposite: attachment. There is no suggestion here of not loving another person; on the contrary, this is the very thing St Teresa is suggesting. What is being criticized is *excessive* love of another person. Excessive love of another person binds the individual to that person. St Teresa is well aware of this, for she says,

> Let us not condescend, oh daughters, to allow our wills to be slaves to anyone, save to the One who bought it [sic] with His blood. Be aware that, without understanding how, you will find yourselves so attached that you will be unable to manage the attachment. Oh, God help me, the silly things that come from such attachment are too numerous to be counted. [4]

What is also perceptive in this passage is that the attachment creeps up on one unawares, so that without knowing it one cannot resist it when resistance is required.

Detachment, which is the same as non-attachment as defined in this book, is dealt with in Chapter 8 of *The Way of Perfection*. Here St Teresa deals with detaching oneself both inwardly and outwardly from all created things, and she does mean *all* created things, for she says, detachment, if it is practised with perfection, includes everything.[5]

This detachment from all created things is, of course, the same idea that is expressed in *The Cloud of Unknowing*, where a 'cloud of forgetting' is to be forged between man and all created things.

In both Chapters 8 and 9 she refers to the attachment to relatives. But in order to understand these comments, and others relating to humility, it is important to realize that there is much evidence that the convent had a definite hierarchy, and some nuns could keep income and other valuables, including pets, while others had rooms to entertain their families[6]. Quarters varied in comfort, and were even traded! Thus, when talking of external attachments she refers explicitly to relatives. It is important that these attachments be broken and left behind when entering the convent, she says, for only then can progress be made to freedom of the spirit. St Teresa obviously felt this to be a major problem, because she continues the theme in Chapter 9, pointing out that,

it is a natural thing for the will to become attached to them [relatives] more than to other persons[7][8].

In commenting on immediate family (parents, brothers and sisters), she points out the difference between being concerned and being attached. She says,

Let us not remain aloof from them if we see that communicating with them does no harm to our religious life. This communication can be carried on with detachment; and so, too, with brothers and sisters.[9]

In trying to understand St Teresa's underlying philosophy it is important to appreciate that she considers everything of this Earth transitory and therefore finite,

> A great aid to going against your will is to bear in mind continually how all is vanity and how quickly everything comes to an end. This helps to remove our attachment to trivia and centre it on what will never end . . . When we begin to become attached to something, we should strive to turn our thoughts from it and bring them back to God. [10]

Not only does this advice provide a motivation for achieving non-attachment, but it also provides a means of achieving it: namely, when thoughts stray, as they inevitably will, then bring them back. The same theme runs throughout most discussions of meditation: it is not easy to keep one's mind focused on a single thought, a single idea; but once one recognizes that the mind has strayed, then bring it back[11].

In the view of St Teresa, however, humility and detachment (non-attachment) go hand in hand. You cannot consider one without the other:

> Here true humility can enter the picture because this virtue and the virtue of detachment it seems to me always go together. They are two inseparable sisters. [12]

In continuing her discussion of these two virtues she makes one of her typically perceptive statements,

> It is true that these virtues [humility and detachment] have the characteristic of so hiding themselves from the person who possesses them that he never sees them or manages to believe that he has them even

though he is told he does. But he esteems them so highly that he always goes about striving to obtain them, and he gradually perfects them within himself. Yet, they are so manifest in the one who possesses them that without his desiring it, these virtues are at once recognized by others who deal with him. [13]

It should be noted that St Teresa does not engage in the allegorical statements typical of St John of the Cross, nor does she use quotations from the scriptures. However, in one rare passage when this is done, we turn to the land of Egypt and the manna in the desert, a theme referred to by St John of the Cross, and one we discuss briefly on p. 135,

> Now, my daughters, this is the work that must be done in order to escape from the land of Egypt, for in finding these virtues you will find the manna. All things will taste good to you. However bad a thing may taste to those who are in the world, you will find it sweet. [14]

We see, then, that St Teresa sees humility and detachment far from being a penance, perceiving them instead as being 'sweet tasting'. What others find burdensome the person with humility and detachment finds a joy. This paradoxical 'joy in adversity' is not as conflicting as it may at first appear. Only in adversity can the ego be subjugated, only in adversity can a person truly find complete detachment. It is a small step from this to the view that mortification is essential, and that mortification of the flesh is probably the most significant,

> Now, then, the first thing we must strive for is to rid ourselves of our love for our bodies. [15]

Thus, in Chapter 10 we find St Teresa's discussion of detachment from the body, especially in minor sickness, and a discussion of mortification. She continues this theme in Chapter 11, where she says that if a sickness is light, don't complain about it; if it is a major sickness then it will reveal its seriousness. And she writes insightfully of the fact that

> A fault this body has is that the more comfort we try to give it the more needs it discovers.[16]

While further on she says,

> . . . when we begin to conquer these wretched little bodies, we will not be so troubled by them.[17]

Although mortification of the flesh is important, as we pointed out earlier, St Teresa discusses *interior mortification*. She implies here that people are basically lazy, and that doing something, no matter what it is, is a bother. Hence, to do something involves an internal conflict[18]. Thus, she says,

> Everything seems to be a heavy burden, and rightly so, because it involves a war against ourselves.[19]

And the way to overcome this is

> by proceeding gradually, not giving in to our own will and appetites, even in little things, until the body is completely surrendered to the spirit.[20]

Once again she emphasizes that the way to achieve these aims is through non-attachment, and by not giving importance to anything that will soon come to an end,

I repeat that the whole matter, or a great part of it, lies in losing concern about ourselves and our own satisfaction . . . In sum, there is no reason to give importance to anything that will come to an end. And who will not work hard if he thinks that each hour is the last? Well, believe me, thinking this is the safest course. [21]

Like St John of the Cross, St Teresa points out that it is necessary constantly to strive against the will in everything. Non-attachment cannot be achieved in one simple step. It is a slow progression through many little trials.

So, let us try hard to go against our own will in everything. For if you are careful, as I said, you will gradually, without knowing how, find yourselves at the summit. [22]

Although this seems to be saying that we should not please ourselves, she points out that pleasure and satisfaction are achieved when we succeed in going against our will. We notice this in our everyday lives. A job has to be done, which we constantly put off. We think that we are getting satisfaction from *not* doing the job we know we must do. Eventually we get round to doing it and we suddenly derive considerable satisfaction from its completion. The burden of the battle is lifted. Unfortunately, we do not appear to learn from this lesson, for the moment a new trial comes along, the moment we must do something we do not want to do, the battle begins anew!

Not only do St Teresa of Avila and St John of the Cross agree with one another, but the same theme runs through other works (religious and non-religious), that is, that great trials can only be achieved if the little ones have been overcome first. Thus, in Chapter 26 St Teresa says,

> So, Sisters, don't think you are capable of such great trials if you are not capable of such little ones. By exercising yourselves in these little trials, you will come to be able to suffer other, greater ones. [23]

This is typical of one of those passages which state an 'obvious truth', one which precisely because it is so 'obvious' tends to go unheeded. But the lessons are there to see. The fact that the solutions are so easy is what makes them that much more difficult!

## THE INTERIOR CASTLE

*The Interior Castle* is undoubtedly St Teresa's best-known work. Written while she was at the Convent of St Joseph of Carmel in Toledo in 1577, it was designed to help her sister nuns solve their difficulties regarding prayer [24]. In this work the path to god is likened to a castle which is composed of seven mansions. The seventh, and most sublime, is where god resides. Outside the castle is darkness and a place seething with toads, vipers and other poisonous vermin. The castle is brightness, and the brightness increases the further into the interior a person progresses. The analogy begins with the First Mansion, where, St Teresa points out, we know our body but not our inner self: we know the rough diamond but not the interior castle,

> It is a shame and unfortunate that through our own fault we don't understand ourselves or know who we are. [25]

Again we see here the importance of knowing the true self, the inner self as referred to by St Teresa. It appears we know much about the body, and even more now than in the time of St Teresa, but we know little about our inner self. Even despite the works of Freud, Jung, Rogers and many others, we still know little about our inner self[26]. Even more significantly, we have little knowledge about the *way* to find out about our inner self. Our modern psychology stresses the ego. In doing this we are kept from knowing about our true self, because the ego is *not* our true self. Modern psychology in fact gives us little guidance as to how to obtain knowledge of our true self – or even of what our true self is. This may, of course, be because psychologists do not accept the distinction!

Of particular importance to St Teresa is how an individual can enter the castle, and this she says can be accomplished through prayer. However, prayer in itself is not enough. Prayer must be accompanied by reflection and meditation[27]. Given her own chosen path this conclusion is not surprising. Whether prayer is the only method of entering the castle or whether there are other methods, the key to the castle is non-attachment, because through non-attachment we can come to know our true self.

But why, then, do people not approach the castle door and try to enter? It is in answering this question that attachment enters St Teresa's argument. People are so preoccupied with a thousand thoughts, each demanding their attention, that they are prevented from reaching the castle door.

> They are so attached to these things that where their treasure lies, their heart goes also.[28]

Although St Teresa does not discuss in detail what these attachments are, there is no doubt that she considers there to be many. Interestingly St Teresa views people as seeing their attachments as 'treasure', and it is their preoccupation with such treasure that prevents them from even thinking about the castle and what it contains.

*The Interior Castle* is strewn with analogies of castles and crystals. St Teresa thinks of the inner self as a crystal. Magnificent though this crystal is, we do not see it: we do not know our inner self. It is as though the crystal were covered over by a black cloth. So long as the cloth remains over the crystal then it does not matter what shines on the individual, they will not know their inner self.

> But if a black cloth is placed over a crystal that is in the sun, obviously the sun's brilliance will have no effect on the crystal even though the sun is shining on it. [29]

To know oneself is to remove the thick black cloth from the crystal. This theme of knowing oneself, of knowing the true self, runs through most of the works discussed in this book. What is so surprising is why we do not seem to know our true selves, and why it is so difficult to do so. In many respects, *The Interior Castle* and many of the other works we are citing are attempts at showing how an individual may achieve a knowledge of his or her true self.

In achieving self-knowledge one of the first steps that a person must take is to achieve humility.

> For humility, like the bee making honey in the beehive, is always at work. Without it, everything goes wrong. [30]

Hence, a person must first enter the room where humility is acquired, for this is the only way to make progress. Unfortunately, the attachments that we have formed make achieving humility difficult.

Terrible are the wiles and deceits used by the devil so that souls may not know themselves or understand their own path. [31]

She continues,

The room is bright but he doesn't enjoy it because of the impediment of things like these wild animals or beasts that make him close his eyes to everything but them. So, I think, must be the condition of the soul. Even though it may not be in a bad state, it is so involved in worldly things and so absorbed with its possessions, honour, or business affairs, as I have said, that even though as a matter of fact it would want to see and enjoy its beauty these things do not allow it to: nor does it seem that it can slip free from so many impediments. [32]

The lesson St Teresa draws from this is that one should avoid looking for trifling faults in others. In order to do this she recommends silence for the individual. It is because we are weak in this first room, therefore, that St Teresa recommends that we call on the help of god and his saints. This may be suitable for a Carmelite nun, to whom St Teresa was specifically addressing herself, but what of the ordinary person today? Certainly the recommendation of not looking for trifling faults in others can be undertaken by everyone and at all times. Silence on the other hand, although possible, is in some senses an escape, and does not prevent negative and destructive thoughts. Although calling on the help of 'God and His saints' will be an approach acceptable to the religious person, there is need of help which takes a different and more practical approach. Even so, there is a view that anyone who wishes to embark on a search for self-realization needs faith.

Furthermore, 'we do not, and cannot, come to self-realization by our own efforts.'[33] Christ put forward the same idea when he said that a person could only reach God through Him,

> I am the way; I am the truth and I am life; no one comes to the Father except by me.
>
> John 14:6

The idea of non-attachment is returned to in her description of the Third Mansion. In particular, she says, the Third Mansion can be achieved by non-attachment, for in

> persevering in this nakedness and detachment from all worldly things he will reach his goal.[34]

Although using the word 'detachment' it is quite clear that St Teresa means it in precisely the same way we have discussed 'non-attachment'. But this quotation says much more. First, it indicates that non-attachment must be undertaken constantly. It is not that you achieve non-attachment and from then on you have it. It is more an attitude towards things. Furthermore, because of human nature being the way it is, ('Terrible are the wiles and deceits used by the devil'), it is very easy to lapse into an attachment to any of the myriad things to which one can become attached. Second, non-attachment is a pre-requisite for reaching the goal: the goal of self-knowledge.

In the second chapter of the Third Mansion, St Teresa returns to the importance of humility, so vital in all her writings:

With humility present, this stage is a most excellent one. If humility is lacking, we will remain here our whole life – and with a thousand afflictions and miseries. For since we will not have abandoned ourselves, this state will be very laborious and burdensome. We shall be walking while weighed down with this mud of our human misery, which is not so with those who ascend to the remaining rooms. [35]

Humility and non-attachment are also brought together in the second chapter of the Fourth Mansion. In this chapter St Teresa gives a very good example of non-attachment in terms of not striving for humility. Humility, although being all important, cannot be struggled for: you cannot strive to achieve humility. But if you do not strive for humility, and humility is so important for progress in the castle's interior, then how is it gained? She answers by saying once again,

I answer that for the following reasons there is no better way than the one I mentioned, of not striving for them. [36]

St Teresa gives five reasons:

1. We should love god without any motive of self-interest.
2. There is a lack of humility if we think by some service we can achieve anything so great.
3. True preparation for receiving these gifts is a desire to suffer, and to imitate the Lord, not to receive consolations.
4. His majesty is not obliged to grant them to us.
5. We should be labouring in vain as the Lord gives it and it cannot be had by labours – meditations, violence to ourselves, the shedding of tears.

And she concludes,

> . . . whoever humbles himself and is detached (I
> mean in fact because the detachment and humility
> must not be just in our thoughts – for they often
> deceive us – but complete) will receive the favour of
> this water from the Lord and many other favours that
> we don't know how to desire. [37]

It is, of course, quite clear from this discussion that
humility and non-attachment are quite different things.
However, humility will not be possible if a person is
attached to worldly things. Hence, non-attachment is a
prerequisite for humility, and humility is a prerequisite for
acquiring true self-knowledge.

Like so many mystics, St Teresa believed that much of
the self-knowledge that we seek is already within us. In
her view, expressed in Chapter 1 of the Fifth Mansion, all
we need to do is ask god's help in finding it. That we
should ask him to

> . . . show us the way and strengthen the soul that it
> may dig until it finds this hidden treasure. The truth
> is that the treasure lies within our very selves. [38]

This view that *the treasure lies within our very selves* runs
through much of the writings of the Spanish mystics and
in the other works discussed in this book.

In talking of the soul in Chapter 1 of the Fifth Mansion,
St Teresa presents ideas very similar to those of Gurdjieff.
Gurdjieff refers to people 'being asleep'. The quotation
marks indicate that he does not mean this in the literal
sense. As we have seen, he meant that people act
mechanically: and in doing so they are asleep! On the
other hand, St Teresa says of the soul,

. . . it only seems that the soul is asleep; for neither does it really think it is asleep nor does it feel awake. There is no need here to use any technique to suspend the mind since all the faculties are asleep in this state – and truly asleep – to the things of the world and to ourselves.[39]

She goes on to say that to love god the soul must withdraw from the body; and so in this Fifth Mansion not imagination nor memory nor understanding can be an obstacle to the blessings that are bestowed on it. Furthermore, it is also necessary to purge the soul,

. . . you now see that God has made this soul a fool with regard to all so as better to impress upon it true wisdom.[40]

Thus it is in this state that god speaks to the soul. The individual has no doubt about this, and even if he never hears it again he can never forget it nor doubt that it happened. What we have here is a statement about the mystical experience. No matter how brief a mystical experience, it impresses itself so completely on a person that he or she can never forget it and cannot doubt that it happened[41].

Because the individual is supposed not to strive, certainly not to strive to achieve humility, and not to make efforts and to achieve a state of non-attachment, then union with god is something which god chooses when the conditions are right. Certainly one of these conditions is the state of non-attachment. St Teresa makes the point forcefully,

But however great the effort we make to do so, we cannot enter. His Majesty must place us there and enter Himself into the centre of our soul. And that He may show His marvels more clearly He doesn't want our will to have any part to play, for it has been entirely surrendered to Him.[42]

In Chapter 2 of the Fifth Mansion we see one of St Teresa's famous analogies, namely that of the silkworm. The silkworm, in forming its cocoon, must be as dead before it can come out as a beautiful white butterfly.

> Let's be quick to do this work and weave this little cocoon by getting rid of our self-love and self-will, our attachment to any earthly thing, and by performing deeds of penance, prayer, mortification, obedience, and of all the other things you know. Would to heaven that we do what we know we must; and we are instructed about what we must do. Let it die; let this silkworm die, as it does in completing what it was created to do! And you will see how we see God, as well as ourselves placed inside His greatness, as in this little silkworm within its cocoon.[43]

She goes on,

> When the soul is, in this prayer, truly dead to the world, a little white butterfly comes forth.[44]

Thus, when the soul communes with god, even for a short time, it comes out as a white butterfly; and as a butterfly, it sets no store on the things it did as a silkworm. Just as the butterfly feels a stranger to the things of the earth, so the soul soars to spiritual heights. Of course, the point is that in order to soar to the spiritual heights the silkworm must die. One way to achieve this death, one way to allow the cocoon to be woven, is to attain non-attachment. It is necessary to remove all attachments that we are prone to have. Of course, being a Carmelite, St Teresa also insists that this course involves penance, prayer, mortification and obedience.

Although *The Interior Castle* continues into Mansions Six and Seven, there is no further discussion of non-attachment. This is how it should be. These later mansions can only be entered after non-attachment has been achieved. Once achieved, there is no reason to consider them further!

**End Notes**

1. *The Collected Works of St Teresa of Avila Volume Two*, translated by Otilio Rodriguez and Kieran Kavanaugh © 1980 by Washington Province of Discalced Carmelites. ICS Publications, 2131 Lincoln Road, N.E., Washington, D.C. 20002, U.S.A., p. 41.
2. The Alumbrados were a group of Spanish *Illuminati* or Perfectionists of the sixteenth century. They particularly emphasized mental prayer.
3. *Life* was withheld from the nuns by Domingo Báñez, her confessor. He would have preferred to burn it rather than have them read it!
4. Rodriguez and Kavanaugh, p. 55.
5. Rodriguez and Kavanaugh, p. 71.
6. Recall the Convent of St Joseph was only partially enclosed and was lax in observing the original Carmelite Rule.
7. Rodriguez and Kavanaugh, p. 74.
8. Attachment to loved ones is also discussed earlier, in Chapter 1, pp. 28–9, indicating that the same basic theme is not restricted to those who take up lives in a convent or monastery.
9. Rodriguez and Kavanaugh, p. 74.
10. Rodriguez and Kavanaugh, p. 76.

11. Recall that exactly the same idea was put forth in *The Cloud of Unknowing*, see p. 81.
12. Rodriguez and Kavanaugh, p. 76.
13. Rodriguez and Kavanaugh, p. 77.
14. Rodriguez and Kavanaugh, p. 77.
15. Rodriguez and Kavanaugh, p. 77.
16. Rodriguez and Kavanaugh, p. 80.
17. Rodriguez and Kavanaugh, p. 81.
18. This interior mortification is almost identical with Gurdjieff's 'yes/no' debate that is necessary to break away from the mechanical sleep in which we find ourselves (see Chapter 2).
19. Rodriguez and Kavanaugh, p. 81.
20. Rodriguez and Kavanaugh, p. 82.
21. Rodriguez and Kavanaugh, p. 82.
22. Rodriguez and Kavanaugh, p. 82.
23. Rodriguez and Kavanaugh, p. 136.
24. Her *Life* was not available to the Carmelite Sisters, and by this time was in the hands of the Inquisitor General.
25. Rodriguez and Kavanaugh, p. 284.
26. We should not confuse, however, knowledge of the unconscious mind with knowledge of the inner self, the true self. They are quite different things.
27. Religions differ largely in their paths to self-enlightenment, although even here there are many similarities. Buddha's eight-fold path to enlightenment (right understanding, right thought, right speech, right action, right livelihood, right effort, right mindfulness and right concentration) is not very far removed from Western Christian teaching.
28. Rodriguez and Kavanaugh, p. 287.
29. Rodriguez and Kavanaugh, p. 289.
30. Rodriguez and Kavanaugh, p. 291.
31. Rodriguez and Kavanaugh, p. 293.
32. Rodriguez and Kavanaugh, p. 294.

33. Johnston, *The Mirror Mind*, p. 32.
34. Rodriguez and Kavanaugh, p. 308.
35. Rodriguez and Kavanaugh, p. 313.
36. Rodriguez and Kavanaugh, p. 326.
37. Rodriguez and Kavanaugh, p. 327.
38. Rodriguez and Kavanaugh, p. 336.
39. Rodriguez and Kavanaugh, p. 336.
40. Rodriguez and Kavanaugh, p. 339.
41. On the mystical experience see R. Woods (ed.) *Understanding Mysticism*, (The Athlone Press, 1981) and W. James, *The Varieties of Religious Experience*, (Penguin, 1982).
42. Rodriguez and Kavanaugh, p. 340.
43. Rodriguez and Kavanaugh, p. 343.
44. Rodriguez and Kavanaugh, p. 343.

# 6

## St John of the Cross

In this chapter we shall discuss two major works of St John of the Cross in relation to non-attachment. It is in these writings that the idea is most fully explained and yet it is nowadays difficult to follow because of our emphasis on material things and strengthening of the ego. It will be noted in the writings we have been discussing, and most particularly the ones we are about to discuss, that they go counter to modern thought on the need for strengthening the ego. This, in itself, may be one of the reasons why today's Church is having great difficulty surviving. But the precepts these and other works express are as relevant today as they were centuries ago. The main difficulty, as I see it, is in making sense of these writings in terms of modern-day life.

It must be realized that many of the religious texts we have been referring to in this and other chapters were not only written *by* religious people, but they were also written *for* religious people. For instance, St John of the Cross was writing for the Carmelite nuns. Because of this, the idea of non-attachment was expressed as a means of achieving union with god. But one of the aims of this book is to demonstrate that non-attachment is a principle on which to base one's life – whether your aim is to live life better, more fully, or to reach your god. Religious people are in agreement over one thing (no matter which religion they

Mount Carmel

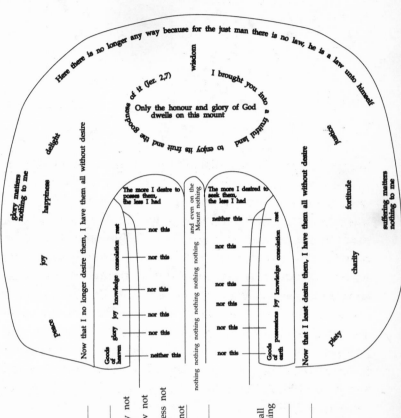

Here there is no longer any way because for the just man there is no law, he is a law unto himself

wisdom

I brought you into a fruitful land to enjoy its fruit and the goodness of it (Jer. 2,7)

Only the honour and glory of God dwells on this mount

justice

peace

fortitude

charity

piety

glory matters nothing to me

happiness

delight

joy

peace

suffering matters nothing to me

Now that I no longer desire them, I have them all without desire

Now that I least desire them, I have them all without desire

The more I desire to possess them, the less I had

Goods of heaven: glory joy knowledge consolation rest

— nor this
— nor this
— nor this
— nor this
— nor this
— neither this

and even on the Mount nothing

nothing nothing nothing nothing nothing nothing

The more I desired to seek them, the less I had

neither this

— nor this
— nor this
— nor this
— nor this
— nor this

Goods of earth: possessions joy knowledge consolation rest

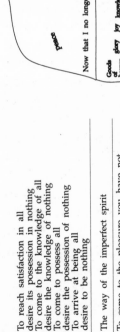

To reach satisfaction in all
desire its possession in nothing
To come to the knowledge of all
desire the knowledge of nothing
To come to possess all
desire the possession of nothing
To arrive at being all
desire to be nothing

The way of the imperfect spirit

To come to the pleasure you have not
you must go by a way in which you enjoy not
To come to the knowledge you have not
you must go by a way in which you know not
To come to the possession you have not
you must go by a way in which you possess not
To come to be what you are not
you must go by a way in which you are not

The path of Mount Carmel the perfect spirit

When you turn toward something
you cease to cast yourself upon the all
for to go from the all to the all
you must leave yourself in all
And when you come to the possession of all
you must possess it without wanting anything

The way of the imperfect spirit

In this nakedness the spirit
finds its rest, for when it
covets nothing, nothing
raises it up, and nothing
weighs it down, because it is
in the center of its humility.

profess), and that is that union with god cannot be achieved unless non-attachment is first achieved. This does, of course, imply attachment to god. But this is the only attachment which is allowed. It is a spiritual attachment. The non-attachment being referred to here is non-attachment to worldly things. The point is

> **non-attachment is only a means of opening oneself up to the glory of god.**

It does not mean that union with god will be automatic; far from it. In the terms used by St Teresa of Avila, non-attachment is a key to the castle, and that is all. The individual has still a long way to go to achieve union with god. We are not concerned here with the journey beyond the door. All we are concerned with is finding the key to open such a door. Without the key, no progress within the castle is possible.

In this chapter we shall discuss two major works of St John of the Cross, *The Ascent of Mount Carmel* and *The Dark Night of the Soul*. Both of these works are made up of a detailed discussion of the following 'stanzas of the soul':

> One dark night,
> Fired with love's urgent longings
> – Ah, the sheer grace! –
> I went out unseen,
> My house being now all stilled;
> In darkness, and secure,
> By the secret ladder, disguised,
> – Ah, the sheer grace! –
> In darkness and concealment,
> My house being now all stilled;
> On that glad night,
> In secret, for no one saw me,

Nor did I look at anything,
With no other light or guide
Than the one that burned in my heart;
This guided me
More surely than the light of noon
To where He waited for me
– Him I knew so well –
In a place where no one else appeared.
O guiding night!
O night more lovely than the dawn!
O night that has united
The Lover with His beloved,
Transforming the beloved in her Lover.
Upon my flowering breast
Which I kept wholly for Him alone,
There He lay sleeping,
And I caressing Him
There in a breeze from the fanning cedars.
When the breeze blew from the turret
Parting His hair,
He wounded my neck
With His gentle hand,
Suspending all my senses.
I abandoned and forgot myself,
Laying my face on my Beloved;
All things ceased; I went out from myself,
Leaving all my cares
Forgotten among the lilies. [1]

However, I begin with a brief biographical sketch of St John
of the Cross.

# ST JOHN OF THE CROSS: A BRIEF BIOGRAPHY

St John of the Cross was born Juan de Yepes y Alvarez in 1542 at Fontiveros, Spain, the youngest of three sons. Soon after his birth the family was reduced to poverty following the death of his father. He later attended the Catechism School (a sort of orphanage for the poor) where he was given an elementary education. While there he was chosen to serve as an acolyte at the Convent of the Augustinian Nuns. At the age of about 17 he began work at the Plague Hospital de la Concepcion, and was allowed to enrol at the Jesuit College in Medina del Campo, where he studied from 1553 to 1563, receiving formal instruction in the humanities. Believing god was calling him to a religious Order, he entered the Carmelite Order at the Monastery of Santa Ana in Medina del Campo in 1563. Little is known about his life as a novitiate there. Later, however, he went to study at his Order's college at Salamanca, there attending lectures at the University of Salamanca, which at the time ranked with those of Bolgna, Paris and Oxford.

He was ordained to the priesthood in 1567. It was in September of that year that he met Madre Teresa of Jesus (that is, St Teresa of Avila), in Medina. It appears he confided in her that he wished to transfer to the Carthusian Order so that he could follow a life of deeper solitude and prayer. She in turn pointed out that he could follow this within a reformed Order amongst the friars. St Teresa took John under her wing, familiarizing him with the daily routine of her nuns[2]. Taking over a farmhouse, a small group of friars, including John, formed the first monastery of friars in the Carmelite Order.

The new life was in keeping with the Primitive Rule of the Order, being largely contemplative. The Rule also required fasts, total abstinence from flesh meat, poverty and withdrawal from the world. They were also to go barefoot (hence the name *Discalced* Carmelites). With the expansion of the Order there was need to educate the young Discalced friars, and this fell to St John of the Cross, who in 1570 was appointed rector of a newly established house of studies in Alcalá. There he guided his students in their studies and spiritual development.

In 1571 St Teresa returned to the Convent of the Incarnation to govern and reform it. In this endeavour she called on the help of St John of the Cross, who was to act as vicar and confessor, including responsibility for the spiritual guidance of St Teresa herself. However, in the years that followed (1572 – 77) a rift began to form between the Mitigated Rule and the Discalced Reform. St John of the Cross became drawn into the conflict, and the Mitigation tried to persuade him to renounce the Reform (i.e., the Carmelite Rule). When this failed he was taken by force and imprisoned in the monastery of the Observance in Avila. It was here that he was confined to a closet, given little food and drink, and flogged three times a week by friars of the Observance. After six months he made a miraculous escape and returned to the Discalced Carmelite nuns. Later he joined the monastery of Monte Calvario, where he was appointed vicar.

After becoming prior of the monastery of El Calvario, he also acted as confessor and spiritual director of the nuns of Beas. It was for these he wrote *The Spiritual Canticle*. After Calvario, St John was to found and become rector of a college for the education of students of the Reform. The years that followed were busy but reasonably calm, and it was during this time that he probably did most of his writing. Troubled times *within* the Reform then followed. The Vicar General of the Discalced called an extraordinary Chapter in June 1590. He had two aims. One was to abandon jurisdiction over the nuns, the other was to expel a member of the Order. Fray John opposed the expulsion. Given the power of the Vicar General, this resulted in John not being appointed to any office the following year. Protests were raised on his behalf, but to no avail. The situation became worse when news spread that he was to be expelled from the Reform. Information was gathered in order to defame John's character, but this gathering of 'evidence' was never completed because Fray John died while it was being compiled. St John of the Cross was beatified in 1675, canonized in 1726 and declared a 'Doctor of the Church' in 1926.

What is quite remarkable is that through all the imprisonments, punishments and persecutions St John remained enlightened. His concern for his fellow-sufferers' physical torments was exceeded only by his concern for their spiritual ones. It was the souls undergoing inner trials that stimulated him to write *The Ascent of Mount Carmel* and *The Dark Night of the Soul*. All his major writing was done in the last 14 years of his life, and it would appear that by the time he had started to write his spiritual synthesis had already been formed in his mind. The result is a consistent set of themes in his writings, which are made up primarily of *The Ascent of Mount Carmel*, *The Dark Night of the Soul*, *The Spiritual Canticle* and *The Living Flame of Love*. His other works consisted of letters and poems, maxims and counsels. Although in this book we will not be discussing his poems, his poetic style still shows through. In fact, the works of St John of the Cross have won him a prominent place in Spanish poetry. His prose is far less stylish. Even so, his works remain an inspiration to many, and have been re-discovered in the Aquarian Age.

# THE ASCENT OF MOUNT CARMEL

St John of the Cross was a Carmelite and mystic, a writer of beautiful simplicity yet with a depth of understanding that is hard to match. He was a prolific writer but one of his most celebrated pieces of work, *The Ascent of Mount Carmel*, is also the work which contains most of his views on non-attachment. He deals with this at length in Book I, where he refers to it as 'the mortification of the appetites and the denial of pleasure in all things'.[3] Only by achieving this, says St John, can a person achieve divine union with god. For if a person is

> Clothed in these affections, a person will be incapable of the enlightenment and dominating fullness of God's pure and simple light, unless he rejects them.[4]

This view is, of course, expressed repeatedly in the Bible – if we take it allegorically, as St John of the Cross did. In the old English Bible we have the famous passage:

> Blessed are the poor in spirit: for theirs is the kingdom of Heaven.
>
> Matt. 5:3

This has always been a difficult passage to interpret[5]. 'Poor in spirit' does not mean 'weak in spirit'; but what does it mean? To detach oneself from things, to be in a position where things have no meaning or importance, requires a strength of spirit. Yet this is the meaning of 'poor in spirit'. In another famous passage we have,

> I repeat, it is easier for a camel to pass through the eye of a needle than for a rich man to enter the kingdom of God.
>
> Matt. 19:24

Here 'rich' does not mean in money and property. But if not, then what does it mean? A person can be rich in knowledge, rich in talent, rich in position and fame. But this often means that the person is attached to such riches, a slave to knowledge, talent, position or whatever. Only by becoming 'poor in spirit', only by becoming non-attached, can a person enter the kingdom of god. In fact, Jesus came to teach disdain of all things, of non-attachment to all things, because only by so doing could a person receive the gift of god's spirit. In Luke, Jesus says[6],

> So also none of you can be a disciple of mine without parting with all his possessions.
>
> Luke 14:33

In the first chapter of this book we discussed the fact that attachment binds a person to that to which he or she is attached. St John goes further, arguing that attachment is a hindrance, that

> . . . attachment to a creature makes a person equal to that creature, the firmer the attachment, the closer is the likeness to the creature, and the greater the equality.[7]

He goes further still. He argues that the person who attaches to a creature is probably lower than that creature rather than its equal because he makes himself a slave to it. Here St John of the Cross is using the word 'creature' to stand for any object, person, idea, etc. as we listed in Figure 1 (p. 26). He is stressing the fact that attachment makes people subservient to the thing to which they are attached. It is this slavish attachment which is a hindrance to seeing things as they really are. And because people in this state cannot see things as they are, they can never see god. Thus,

A man who is in darkness does not comprehend the light, so neither will a person attached to creatures be able to comprehend God. Until a man is purged of his attachments he will not be equipped to possess God, neither here below through the pure transformation of love, nor in heaven through the beatific vision.[8]

St John of the Cross argues that this is the interpretation of the heavenly manna given the Israelites in the Biblical Book of Exodus. The children of Israel did not receive manna until the flour they had brought from Egypt was all gone. In other words, they had first to renounce, to become non-attached. Only by becoming non-attached could they savour the word of god. When they ate both meat and manna they co-mingled the base with one higher. The craving for meat is meant to represent attachment, and that such attachment was anathema to god. Thus, St John says,

. . . he who loves something together with God undoubtedly makes little of God for he weighs in the balance with God an object far distant from God.[9]

The attachment to an object and mistakenly equating that object with something higher is stated yet again, more forcefully,

It is the common knowledge of experience that when the will is attached to an object, it esteems that object higher than any other, even though another, not as pleasing, may deserve higher admiration. And if a man desires pleasure from both objects, he is necessarily offensive to the more deserving, because through his desire for both he equates the two. Since nothing equals God, a person who loves and is attached to something other than God, or together with Him, offends God exceedingly. If this be true, what would happen if he loved something more than God?[10]

It will be noted that St John of the Cross does not take the Bible literally. On the contrary, he considers it in a purely allegorical sense. Accordingly, he interprets Moses' climb to the top of Mount Sinai (Exod. 34:1–3), where he was instructed to leave the children of Israel below and not pasture beasts on the mountainside, as meaning that a person must renounce all things and must not attach himself to anything that is not purely god if he is to reach god. For a person to reach god,

> . . . necessarily demands a habitual effort to renounce and mortify the appetites; the sooner this mortification is achieved, the sooner the soul reaches the top. But until the appetites are eliminated, a person will not arrive, no matter how much virtue he practices [*sic*]. For he will fail to acquire perfect virtue, which lies in keeping the soul empty, naked, and purified of every appetite.[11]

A similar point is expressed by St John of the Cross when commenting on the angel's request to Tobias to wait three nights before having any union with his bride (Tobit 6:8 – 12)[12]. It is the first of the three nights which refers to non-attachment. On this night Tobias was to burn the fish heart in the fire. Of this St John of the Cross says,

> That heart symbolized the human heart that is attached to worldly things. To undertake the journey to God the heart must be burned and purified of all creatures with the fire of divine love.[13]

The point being expressed in all these quotations and interpretations of the scriptures is that in order to undertake the journey to god, in order to achieve perfect virtue, a person must *first* achieve non-attachment. What must not be over-looked is that non-attachment comes first.

St John of the Cross substantiates all his views with interpretations of the scriptures. Not only does the Bible emphasize the importance of non-attachment, but it also gives the method by which to achieve it. This is given in Genesis, where god instructs Jacob to go to Bethel and there to build an altar. But Jacob first says to his people,

> Rid yourselves of the foreign gods which you have among you, purify yourselves, and see your clothes are mended.
>
> Gen. 35:2

In other words, a person must first cast out all attachments and affections (all foreign gods). The only affection, the only attachment, is to god. Second, he or she must develop the habit of denying attachments (in order to purify the spirit). Third, having achieved the first two, the soul must obtain a new understanding of god (a mended set of clothes)[14]. The first is merely a statement. The second, however, is the method for achieving non-attachment. It is done by denying attachments – big and small. Purification is not an immediate act, it is, rather, a long process of observing oneself and noting the attachments that one has and constantly denying them.

Attachments cause two main problems, says St John of the Cross:

1. they deprive the person of god's spirit; and
2. they weary, torment, darken, defile and weaken him.

In justifying the first he repeatedly makes the point that two contraries cannot co-exist in the same object. Consequently, the old must be purged from him for the new to enter.

> In natural generation a new form cannot be introduced
> into a subject without expulsion of the form already
> there, which is an impediment to the new form
> because of the existing contrariety. Similarly, insofar as
> a person is subject to a sensory form, an entirely
> spiritual one cannot enter him. [15]

He goes on to explain this second point in some detail.
Attachment is wearisome because it resembles a child who
is restless, hard to please and never satisfied; like a man
digging for treasure; like someone with a fever; like the
wind which disturbs water; and so on. It torments and
afflicts just as does torture in a rack or lying naked on
thorns and nails. He argues that the result of the torment
is as great as the appetite (attachment), and the greater the
number of attachments the greater the torment.
Attachment darkens and blinds a man just as vapours make
the air murky and a hindrance to bright sunshine; like a
mirror that is cloudy and so does not reflect clearly a
person's countenance. This darkening of the intellect
weakens the will and makes the memory dull and
disordered. The attachment blinds and darkens the soul
because it is itself blind,

> . . . if one blind man guides another they will both fall
> into the ditch.
>
> Matt. 15:4

Furthermore, attachment defiles the soul. Just as liquid is
polluted if mud is mixed with it, so attachment makes a
person similar to that to which he or she is attached and
so pollutes and defiles the soul. Finally, attachment
weakens a person by sapping the strength needed for
perseverance in the practice of virtue.

It is not simply that attachment weakens a person, but that attachment becomes self-fulfilling. The more one becomes attached the more the desire for the object of attachment increases, and the more a person becomes burdened. As attachment grows, the burden grows and so does sorrow and dissatisfaction. We find this expressed in Job,

> Because his appetite gave him no rest,
> and he cannot escape his own desires,
> nothing is left for him to eat,
> and so his well-being does not last;
> with every need satisfied his troubles begin and the
> full force of his hardship strikes him.
>
> Job 20:0–22

St John of the Cross argues that all voluntary attachments must be eliminated. No matter how small the attachment it will make progress to perfection impossible – just as a bird tied by a thin thread or by a cord cannot fly off. Although one may conquer strong attachments, one is still bound if one has even the most simple childish attachment. This can hinder advancement in the same way that a small crack in a pitcher of water which goes unrepaired can lead to the loss of all liquid. This complete purging of *all* attachments is the interpretation given to what Joshua had to do before entering the city of Jericho, where everything was to be destroyed (Josh. 6:18 – 21). Of this St John says,

> The lesson here is that all objects living in the soul –
> whether they be many or few, large or small – must
> die in order that the soul enter divine union, and it
> must bear no desire for them but remain detached as
> though they were nonexistent to it, and it to them. [16]

He further adds that by the practice of one virtue, all virtues grow; but equally, through an increase in one vice, all the vices and their effects grow.

St John gives three means by which to conquer the appetites, of which he says,

> [They] are as profitable and efficacious as they are concise. He who sincerely wants to practice [sic] them will need no others, since all the others are included in these.

They are:

1. Have an habitual desire to imitate Christ.
2. Renounce and remain empty of any sensory satisfaction that is not purely for the honour and glory of God.
3. Always be inclined:
   not to the easiest, but to the most difficult;
   not the most delightful, but to the harshest;
   not to the most gratifying, but to the less pleasant;
   not to the consoling, but to the unconsoling;
   not to the most, but to the least;
   not to the highest and most precious, but to the lowest and most despised;
   not to wanting something, but to wanting nothing;
   do not go about looking for the best of temporal things, but for the worst;
   and desire to enter for Christ into complete nudity, emptiness, and poverty in everything in the world. [17]

St John of the Cross also gives a fourth measure, by which to overcome pride;

4. Act with contempt for yourself and desire all others do likewise; speak in contempt of yourself and desire all

others to do likewise; and try to think lowly and contemptuously of yourself and desire all others to do the same.[18]

St John of the Cross concludes this counsel with the verses set out to accompany the drawing of *The Ascent of Mount Carmel*, reproduced at the opening of this chapter (see p. 127).

To reach satisfaction in all
desire its possession in nothing.
To come to possess all
desire the possession of nothing.
To arrive at being all
desire to be nothing.
To come to the knowledge of all
desire the knowledge of nothing.
To come to the pleasure you have not
you must go by a way in which you enjoy not.
To come to the knowledge you have not
you must go by a way in which you know not.
To come to the possession you have not
you must go by a way in which you possess not.
To come to be what you are not
you must go by a way in which you are not.
When you turn toward something
you cease to caste yourself upon the all.
For to go from all to the all
you must deny yourself of all in all.
And when you come to the possession of the all
you must possess it without wanting anything.
Because if you desire to have something in all
your treasure in God is not purely your all.
In this nakedness the spirit finds
its quietude and rest.

For in coveting nothing
nothing raises it up
and nothing weighs it down,
because it is in the centre of its humility.
When it covets something
in this very desire it is wearied.[19]

In these lines St John of the Cross not only sums up his whole philosophy but provides a very practical guide on how to attain non-attachment. More than that, he provides a key to achieving union with god. In these lines we see not only St John's depth of understanding, but also his ability to write beautiful verse.

## THE DARK NIGHT

St John of the Cross returns to the idea of non-attachment in his work, *The Dark Night of the Soul*. It must be recalled that St John of the Cross wrote this for his Carmelite sisters. He says of novices that 'they weigh themselves down with overly decorated images and rosaries'[20]. Hence, he is again pointing out the problem of attachment. He says,

What I condemn in this is possessiveness of heart and attachment to the number, workmanship, and overdecoration of these objects. For this attachment is contrary to poverty of spirit which is intent only upon the substance of the devotion, benefits by no more than what procures this sufficiently, and tires of all this other multiplicity and elaborate ornamentation. Since true devotion comes from the heart and looks only to the truth and substance represented by spiritual objects, and since everything else is imperfect attachment and possessiveness, any appetite for these things must be uprooted if some degree of perfection is to be reached. [21]

When discussing the first stanza of *The Dark Night of the Soul* he returns to the point about attachment forming a bond between the person and the thing to which he or she is attached. Furthermore, the bond is stronger the stronger the attachment. He says,

> For when the appetite is allowed indulgence in some imperfection, the soul immediately feels an inclination towards it, little or great in proportion to the degree of its satisfaction and attachment. [22]

St John of the Cross argues that the allegorical meaning of god's instruction to Moses to take off his shoes (Exod. 3:4–5) denotes not only respect and discretion when communing with god, but also 'the nakedness of appetite'. Leaving behind his shoes represents leaving behind his attachments and the things which gratify. This denial of attachment is seen by St John of the Cross to be very important,

> When the sensory appetites, gratifications, and supports are quenched, the intellect is left limpid and free to understand the truth, for even though these concern spiritual things they blind and impede the spirit. [23]

He then returns to the topic of even one attachment being a hindrance, which he discussed in *The Ascent of Mount Carmel*. He says,

> Only one attachment or only one particular object to which the spirit is actually or habitually bound is

enough to hinder the experience or reception of the delicate and intimate delight of the spirit of the love which contains eminently in itself all delights. [24]

The reason, as he constantly points out in all his writings, is that two contraries cannot co-exist in one subject. Darkness and light cannot co-exist. St John likens darkness to attachments and lightness to god's spirit. A person cannot have both attachments and the light of divine union. In order, therefore, to allow in the light of divine union it is necessary to eliminate the darkness, it is necessary to purge oneself of attachments.

In one of his most perceptive passages, St John of the Cross explains why many people will refuse to achieve non-attachment. In this passage he is discussing the similarity of the attainment of secret wisdom with the ladder of Jacob[25]. He says,

> The secrecy of this ascent is evident since ordinarily the losing and annihilation of the self, which brings most profit to a man, will be considered the worst for him, whereas consolation and satisfaction (which are the less value and ordinarily involving loss rather than gain if attachment is involved) will be considered the best. [26]

We see here what has become recognized by many. The wisdom contained in the Bible (and many other works in all religions) is often rejected. The conclusion one comes to is the importance of achieving non-attachment. For those of a religious disposition, only by achieving non-attachment will they receive and understand god's message:

Who is it that the prophet hopes to teach,

to whom will what they hear make sense?
Are they babes newly weaned, just taken from
   the breast?

Isa. 28:9

## CONCLUSION

In these two works by St John of the Cross we see the culmination of medieval thought on the topic of non-attachment. Not only do these medieval works indicate the importance of non-attachment, but they also provide ways of achieving it. In the next and final chapter, the lessons we can learn from these medieval works, and those discussed in Chapter 2, are brought together. Chapter 7 also provides exercises that can be done to help your progress in achieving non-attachment.

### End Notes

1. *The Collected Works of St John of the Cross*, translated by Kieran Kavanaugh and Otilio Rodriguez © 1979 by Washington Province of Discalced Carmelites. ICS Publications, 2131 Lincoln Road, N.E., Washington, D.C. 20002, U.S.A., pp. 295–6.
2. St John of the Cross was a small man, only about 5' tall, and St Teresa often called him 'little Seneca' or 'the holy little Fray John'.
3. Kavanaugh and Rodriguez, p. 77.
4. Kavanaugh and Rodriguez, pp. 77–8.
5. This is the *New English Bible*, (Oxford University Press, 1970) version:

    'How blest are those who know their need of God; the kingdom of Heaven is theirs.'

    Note how this replaces the phrase 'poor in spirit'. No doubt this is in part because the phrase is difficult to interpret. Here we have interpreted it to mean non-attachment, which is not unreasonable.

6. Once again there is something lost in the *New English Bible* version. The older version has it as:

'He who does not renounce all that he possesses with his will cannot be my disciple.'

What is lost in the newer edition is the phrase 'with his will', which emphasizes the very attachment with which we have been dealing.

7. Kavanaugh and Rodriguez, p. 78.

8. Kavanaugh and Rodriguez, p. 78.

9. Kavanaugh and Rodriguez, p. 82.

10. Kavanaugh and Rodriguez, p. 82–3.

11. Kavanaugh and Rodriguez, p. 83.

12. Tobit, the book in the Apocrypha of the *New English Bible*, has no mention of Tobias' three nights, although there is a clear reference to the fish heart.

13. Kavanaugh and Rodriguez, p. 75

14. The three things referred to in Genesis 35:2 are very similar to those of Tobias' three nights, but see note 12, above.

15. Kavanaugh and Rodriguez, p. 85.

16. Kavanaugh and Rodriguez, p. 99.

17. Kavanaugh and Rodriguez, pp. 102–3.

13. Kavanaugh and Rodriguez, p. 103.

19. Kavanaugh and Rodriguez, pp. 103–4.

20. Kavanaugh and Rodriguez, p. 302.

21. Kavanaugh and Rodriguez, p. 302.

22. Kavanaugh and Rodriguez, p. 313.

23. Kavanaugh and Rodriguez, p. 322.

24. Kavanaugh and Rodriguez, p. 346.

25. Jacob was on his way from Beersheba to Harran when he bedded down for the night. 'He dreamt that he saw a ladder, which rested on the ground with its top reaching to heaven, and angels of God were going up and down upon it.' (Gen. 28:12).

26. Kavanaugh and Rodriguez, p. 375.

# 7

## Lessons and Exercises

Lessons

The need to achieve non-attachment in the Aquarian Age is essential. In this chapter, therefore, we shall bring together a number of lessons (86 in all) which can be extracted from the works we have been looking at. In doing this I have either taken the text as it is when it is expressed in straightforward English, or I have 'translated' the text into simpler, more modern English.

The purpose of doing this is two-fold. First, seeing the lessons in their entirety and without embellishments gives them a greater impact. Second, they provide a quick reference guide, since I have also appended to each lesson the chapter from which it is taken. These lessons, however, only indicate the importance of non-attachment and *why* a person should achieve it. What they do not do is explain *how* to achieve non-attachment. This then is the purpose of the exercises (14 in all). I have tried in these exercises to bring together techniques for achieving non-attachment which have been revealed or suggested in the works discussed. In some cases I have expanded on these in order to make them 'truly' exercises.

## LESSONS

1. We can get some idea of non-attachment by behaving in such a way that the ego is reduced. In doing this a person will come to realize something is different within him- or herself. In other words, the deliberate change in behaviour must elicit a change in subjective feeling and attitudes. (Chapter 1)

2. Non-attachment implies a weakening of the ego. (Chapter 1)

3. Ego-centred behaviour is neither the only behaviour nor necessarily the most appropriate one for society. (Chapter 1)

4. A society which is based on co-operation rather than conflict is one for which non-attachment will be a central concept. (Chapter 1)

5. The techniques may be universal. It is only the context in which they are performed (the myth) which is different. (Chapter 1)

6. Loss of ego must be a first step, and this can only be achieved by an individual's own efforts, and through a process of non-attachment. (Chapter 1)
7. Non-attachment is not for everyone. (Chapter 1)
8. Non-attachment is none of the following:
   (a) detachment,
   (b) unconcern about things,    -
   (c) unresponsiveness or coldness,
   (d) indifference. (Chapter 1)
9. Non-attachment is the absence of attachment. (Chapter 1)
10. Attachment to something – an object, an activity, a person, an idea, a profession, a philosophy, a place or some period of time – means that you are subservient to that object, that activity, that person, idea, profession, philosophy, place or period of time. Your behaviour is not unconditional, but rather conditioned by the thing to which you are attached. (Chapter 1)
11. Attachment creates an emotional bond between a person and the thing to which he or she is attached. (Chapter 1)
12. Attachment goes *from the person to the object*. The person *chooses* to become attached to the object. (Chapter 1)
13. Non-attachment is the absence of any slavish connection with an object, an activity, a person, an idea, a job, a philosophy, a place, or a time. (Chapter 1)
14. A person may be non-attached to just some things and not others. For instance, you may have no attachment to objects, activities, job, place, or time, but may be attached to another person, or to an idea or philosophy. (Chapter 1)
15. Individuals have a dynamic existence, and will change over time. Non-attachment may be achieved but it can also be lost. (Chapter 1)
16. Non-attachment lets you live life to the full. (Chapter 1)

17. Something can be *known* at either an intellectual or at an emotional level, but to *understand* something requires that it be known at *both* the intellectual and emotional levels. (Chapter 1)

18. A person *first* responds emotionally and *then* intellectualizes about the response. (Chapter 1)

19. The emotional centre responds more quickly than does the intellectual centre. (Chapter 1)

20. The importance of non-attachment cannot be understood unless it is appreciated at both the intellectual and the emotional levels. (Chapter 1)

21. A non-attached person does not let his or her emotions rule. (Chapter 1)

22. Mortification is a means of achieving non-attachment, but *excessive* mortification is a form of attachment. (Chapter 1)

23. New neural pathways in the brain can only be made if an individual does something new. This something new must be *active*. Mortification is just one method of creating a new neural pathway. (Chapter 1)

24. 'Everyday' mortification can be undertaken simply by engaging in self-denials, which should be inconspicuous, non-competitive and not injurious to health. (Chapter 1)

25. An individual cannot *do* anything, he or she merely responds to the influences placed upon him or her. (Chapter 2)

26. Each of us is composed of many 'I's'. You must divide yourself into two: into the observing and the observed. You can never change yourself from where you are presently unless you can accept this division. (Chapter 2)

27. A person is born with *essence* and around this grows *personality*. The way to allow essence to grow is to make personality passive. To make personality passive, a

person must engage in non-identifying (non-attachment). (Chapter 2)

28. Personality can be made passive by self-observation. (Chapter 2)

29. Essence can be stimulated to grow only by introducing 'friction' i.e., by becoming involved in the conscious struggle between 'yes' and 'no'. (Chapter 2)

30. Each individual is composed of three centres: the physical, the emotional and the intellectual centres. Each centre can become involved in the yes/no struggle. (Chapter 2)

31. Transformation of an individual requires a 'first conscious shock'. Non-identifying (non-attachment) is what supplies this first conscious shock. (Chapter 2)

32. The individual has four bodies. For most only the physical body is developed. In this case the person is mechanical, simply responding to life's stimuli. The development of essence allows some of the other bodies to develop and allows the causation to be reversed, i.e., allows the inner person to dictate which influence he or she wishes to respond to and in what way. (Chapter 2 and Appendix)

33. In order for a person to be reborn he or she must first awaken. The sequence of events is awakening, death and rebirth. (Chapter 2)

34. The *fourth way* requires no renunciation of ordinary life, but it must be found. (Chapter 2)

35. The *fourth way* requires progress to be made on all three centres simultaneously: the physical, emotional, and intellectual. (Chapter 2)

36. The *fourth way* involves knowing yourself, your true self. (Chapter 2)

37. The more someone understands what he or she is doing, the greater will be the results of his or her efforts. (Chapter 2)

38. Whatever we identify with at once has power over us, and the more often we identify with something, the more we are slaves to it. (Chapter 2)
39. To break away from one attachment will lead to the creation of another. One must come to a position where one is able to *choose* to which influence one wishes to become attached. (Chapter 2)
40. Force can be lost, gained or created. Non-attachment prevents the loss of force. Every act of non-attachment saves force. Such acts of non-attachment, and the resulting saving of force, must be carried out throughout one's life. (Chapter 2)
41. Each person must engage in his or her own yes/no conflicts, and as such everything is *relative* and particular to the individual. (Chapter 2)
42. Yes/no conflicts must be engaged in consciously; unconscious conflicts are wasteful and not part of the development process. (Chapter 2)
43. See what you still lack, not what you have already; for that is the quickest way of getting and keeping humility. (Chapter 3)
44. On occasion forget about things and their purpose, try not to attach yourself to things and try to pay them no attention. (Chapter 3)
45. Non-attachment is necessary in order to know the true self. (Chapter 3)
46. Attachments are a problem because they occupy your thoughts most of the time; and the more you like something the more you attach yourself to it and the more time you spend thinking about it. (Chapter 3)
47. Magic creates attachments, while religion breaks them down. (Chapter 3)
48. Attachments tend to give pleasure and delight, and because of this a person dwells on them, paying them attention at the expense of other things. (Chapter 3)

49. Humility is nothing else but a true knowledge and awareness of oneself as one really is. (Chapter 3)

50. To know god a person must acquire self-knowledge. (Chapter 4)

51. A person must resist sin, and must be constantly watchful over his or her emotions and innermost thoughts. Only by self-examination can the individual realize the extent of his or her sin in word, deed or thought. It is impossible to escape from sin, and so a person must constantly struggle against it, and in the struggle he or she must constantly suffer. (Chapter 4)

52. A person who can achieve non-attachment achieves humility. He or she also acquires a quietness and joy which can be preserved no matter what is going on externally. (Chapter 4)

53. A person must be dead of self, i.e., must achieve non-attachment to worldly things. The person who is not dead of self is easily tempted, and will be defeated by small and petty things. (Chapter 4)

54. The highest and most profitable form of study is to understand one's inmost nature and despise it; real wisdom and perfection lie in having no high opinion of oneself, but in always thinking highly of others. (Chapter 4)

55. No one has a harder struggle than the person who is striving to overcome him- or herself. (Chapter 4)

56. Facing difficulties and opposition is good because it brings one back towards one's true self. It is even more important to overcome things that one is attached to. It is easy to overcome the things that one is not attached to. (Chapter 4)

57. The man who is living the inward life can soon still all his thoughts, because he never abandons himself entirely to outward things. No physical toil is any obstacle to him, nor any activity that must be

performed – he can adjust to anything that comes. (Chapter 4)

58. There are only a few contemplatives because only a few individuals know how to achieve non-attachment. (Chapter 4)

59. Non-attachment is a form of surrender. It must be done throughout life, both in small things and in large things. It must also be done thoroughly and honestly. (Chapter 4)

60. Humility encompasses non-attachment. You can only have true humility if you are non-attached. (Chapter 5)

61. Attachments tend to creep up on a person, so that when resistance to an attachment is required it cannot be achieved. (Chapter 5)

62. Non-attachment, if it is practised with perfection, includes everything. (Chapter 5)

63. Everything in life is transient. It is not useful, therefore, to attach yourself to such transient and therefore unimportant things. (Chapter 5)

64. Since non-attachment is almost impossible and must constantly be strived for, then it is necessary constantly to attempt to achieve it, and by so doing perfect it within oneself. (Chapter 5)

65. The first thing we must strive for is to rid ourselves of our love for our bodies. This is important, because the more comfort we give the body the more it craves further comforting. (Chapter 5)

66. Non-attachment must be achieved in all things, proceeding gradually from little attachments on to big ones. This inevitably involves a war against oneself. We can only achieve non-attachment in big trials if we first achieve them in little ones. (Chapter 5)

67. We know much about the body but little about our inner self. What is more, we know little about the way in which to find out about our inner self. (Chapter 5)

68. Attachments, and there are many, prevent one from finding one's true self because they distract one to too great an extent. (Chapter 5)

69. So long as our attachments distract us from our true self, then it does not matter what information we read, hear or see concerning our true self, we will not take any notice of it because our attention will be occupied elsewhere. (Chapter 5)

70. We cannot come to self-realization by our own efforts. (Chapter 5)

71. Self-knowledge will reveal itself at the appropriate time; this time cannot be chosen by the individual. (Chapter 5)

72. Just as the silkworm must die in order to transform into a butterfly, and just as the butterfly is a stranger to things of the Earth, so each of us must die of self if we are to transform into something of the spirit. (Chapter 5)

73. Only by achieving non-attachment is divine union with god possible. (Chapter 6)

74. Attachment to something makes a person equal to that thing, and the firmer the attachment the closer the likeness. (Chapter 6)

75. Slavish attachments prevent a person from seeing things as they truly are. (Chapter 6)

76. If a person has attachments to two or more things then he or she will equate the two. If, however, one is more deserving than the other, then this equating is necessarily offensive to the object or person more deserving of the person's attachment. (Chapter 6)

77. Non-attachment requires continued effort; only absolute non-attachment will lead to perfect virtue, no matter how much virtue a person presently practises. To achieve perfect virtue, non-attachment must first be attained. (Chapter 6)

78. Purification is not an immediate act, rather it is a long process of observing oneself, noting the attachments that one has, and constantly denying them. (Chapter 6)

79. Two opposites cannot co-exist within the same object. Hence, to accept a new element then an old one must first be eliminated (purged). While a person is attached to the body and all the sensory elements that this entails, then it is not possible for spiritual entities to enter. (Chapter 6)

80. Attachments never appear satisfied. The stronger the attachment, or the greater number of attachments, then the greater is the battle in overcoming them. (Chapter 6)

81. The more a person becomes attached to something the more he or she desires it. (Chapter 6)

82. All attachments must be eliminated. Even if a person eliminates the strong attachments, so long as one little attachment remains advancement is hindered. [A small crack in a pitcher of water can still lead to the loss of *all* the water.] (Chapter 6)

83. The practice of one virtue leads to the growth of all virtues; however, the increase in one vice means the growth of all vices. (Chapter 6)

84. The verses in St John's *The Ascent of Mount Carmel* indicate that people must not only strive to attain non-attachment, but that they must *actively* change from what they presently do and think. (Chapter 6)

85. Although the greatest gain comes from the loss of self (non-attachment), an individual will consider it the worst possible course because of the battle which it entails; while submission to attachments will be considered the best possible course, even though it is the worst, because it leads to pleasure. (Chapter 6)

86. Secret wisdom is most usually rejected. (Chapter 6)

# EXERCISES

In these exercises I have drawn only partially on the works discussed in this book; they are, however, the basis for the exercises. Since my intention is to make them very practical exercises, I include in each exercise a discussion of what is going on, and on which text (if any) it is based. Although the exercises follow the order of the chapters, they can be practised in any sequence or combination.

## Exercise 1

A major feature of the Gurdjieffian system is to know yourself. To do this you must observe yourself. In doing this, however, you must also distinguish *events* from *states*. Events take place outside yourself, they influence you, and can be good or bad. States, on the other hand, refer to your inner world: how you respond to events, how you think about events, your mood, etc. In general events cannot be changed. What can be changed are states.

This exercise is made up of two parts. The first part is simply to record consciously the way in which you respond to events. If necessary take note of your responses. Note which responses you found good, which bad, which pleasant and which unpleasant. Which led you to worry and which you could just ignore? And so on.

The events that take place throughout the day supply a vast amount of information about us if we make a conscious effort to observe our mechanical responses to them. The aim is not to catalogue the events *per se* but rather to catalogue your responses to them. What you are establishing is categories, such as your 'laziness response', your 'anger response', your 'morning response', your response to criticism, to illness, to good (bad) news, and so on.

The second part of the exercise is to consider whether you are experiencing the *correct* response to events. This is not easy to do, because it begs the question: what is the correct response to events? Suppose some event happens to you. You may respond to it with your 'anger response' or with your 'surprise response' or with your 'bad news response'. The question is, which response is the most appropriate? If you think this strange, imagine that you are going into your house. You may enter through the front door, through the back door, through the window or down the chimney. Even if you enter through the front door, you may enter by means of a key or by breaking down the door. In this case the 'correct' response is not so difficult to recognize. Why is it, then, so difficult to see which response we should adopt for events in life? It is because we have not consciously thought about which response we should have to any event. We simply respond, and respond mechanically.

Even a correct response on one occasion may not be the correct response on another occasion. Returning to the analogy of entering your house, you may consider the 'right' response that of entering by the front door with your key. But suppose you left your key inside, but then remembered that the back door was unlocked. Then the 'right' response would be to enter the house through the back door. Here, of course, the event is somewhat different; or alternatively, the environmental conditions within which the event took place are different. The point again being made is that the 'right' response to events depends on the event and on the environmental conditions in which the event occurs. So too with the 'right' internal response.

## Exercise 2

This next exercise is a way to consider whether you are a single 'I'. Once you recognize that you have multiple 'I's', then the next stage is to consider how contradictory are these different 'I's' and what it is that allows such contradictions to remain.

First consider a time when you made a resolve to do something and then never did it. Was this because you changed your mind, or because you were lazy, or because the 'I' that made the resolve was not the 'I' who would have to carry it out? We all go through times when we plan to do something and then do not do it. It can be a simple thing like putting a book back on the shelf, or washing the clothes, or going to visit someone we know. Although it is easy to say that the reason we do not do it is we are lazy (which may be true), it is also possible that we are a collection of different 'I's', and that the 'I' who made the resolve is not the 'I' who has to implement it. Again, to make the point with another example, it is often true that, having drunk a sufficient amount of alcohol, we make plans to get 'this or that' done the next day. When the next day comes, however, the 'this or that' never gets done. We may blame the alcohol[1], but another interpretation is that the inebriated 'I' is the one making all the plans, while it is the sober 'I' who has to carry them out, and decides not to.

The first stage of this exercise is simply to note the occasions on which we make plans or resolutions. In noting them it is important to attempt to establish the characteristics of the 'I' who is making the decision, as well as of the 'I' who is then not accomplishing it. Even if a decision *is* carried out, this too should be observed in order to see whether it is the same 'I' making and effecting the decision.

The most important aspects of our different 'I's' will, however, be discovered when we observe those situations in which our resolutions are *not* carried out. Why is this? It is because these situations help you to learn not only about the different 'I's', but also about the internal *buffers* which you have built up over the course of your lifetime which allow the distinct 'I's' to co-exist even when they are contradictory. Typical buffers one tends to employ are: avoiding unpleasant situations, lying or deluding oneself, blaming others rather than oneself, finding fault in others, self-justification, criticizing others, and so on. The list is quite long, and the older you are the more buffers you have created by means of your 'false personality'[2].

It is necessary to observe the buffers in action. Some buffers in particular divide two emotional extremes, for example pleasant from unpleasant feelings, or likes from dislikes. It is important with such buffers to see both sides of the buffer *simultaneously*. Only by seeing both sides at once can you see the contradictions within your different 'I's'. It is very much like being able to see both sides of an argument. One person argues that A is right. Another person argues that B is right. Usually, each person can see only his or her own point of view. What is being suggested here is to see both A and B simultaneously. Whether A is right or B is right is not at issue, the object is to see both points of view simultaneously. The everyday expression for doing this – and its importance is therefore recognized although it tends to go unheeded – is 'to put yourself in the other person's shoes'.

The reason why this exercise is not easy is that we all create buffers in order to make life easy, to make it tolerable, to make it understandable. According to the Gurdjieffian system, however, such buffers prevent the true development of the individual. The only thing that will allow an individual to develop is a shock. Only when a person *realizes* something about him or herself does he or she develop. It is this *realization* which occurs through shocks. Of course, the purpose of buffers is to lessen or reduce shocks. Buffers therefore prevent us from truly developing. What they do allow is the development of *false personality*.

The purpose of this exercise is to give you a full, conscious understanding of the way in which you act and respond, and exactly what attitude you are adopting about something: are you lying, engaging in self-justification, or being negative? This exercise can be seen as a means of achieving inner sincerity.

**Exercise 3**

In this brief exercise the aim is more general, and is a question of attitude.

There is a tendency to live life as a series of events. An alternative is to see life as a school, as a means of learning more about one's true self. Life is the teacher and you are the pupil. In this relationship, unlike that of traditional schooling, the teacher-pupil relationship is never-ending; it goes on throughout one's life. Every situation, each event offers you some insight: you can learn from the grimace that crosses your face in response to something just as from your reactions to the death of someone you know intimately. Everything you do or do not do in life will supply information about your being.

A more positive and simple feature of this exercise is to take one hour every day and consciously observe yourself during that hour. Do not let anything you do or think go by without observing it; being all the while fully aware of yourself doing or thinking it. This is not as easy as it may sound. So much of what we do is mechanical that being consciously aware for one hour will, in the first instance, be an impossibility. But with practice you will become more and more proficient at it.

## Exercise 4

This exercise is meant to help you understand your negativity.

It is first necessary to accept that you are negative in many ways. Second, it is necessary to observe on which occasions you are negative. In this observation it is important to realize that in general it takes the presence of another person to make you feel negative, but that this negativity comes from within yourself; only you produce your own negativity. When you respond negatively in the presence of another, you must ask yourself three questions:

1. Do I consider that I am being badly treated?
2. Am I jealous?
3. Is my negative response purely mechanical?

You must then consider your response in all its facets.

The next part of the exercise is to put yourself in the other person's situation. Even more, *become* the other person. Once you have done this, which admittedly is not easy, you must then consider how you look from the point of view of this other person in whose shoes you are now standing. In other words, you must take an extended look at yourself, but from the vantage point of the person who is making you feel so negative. This is painful, because the object is to see yourself as others see you. The exercise also requires the skill of visualization, in order to truly become the other person[3].

**Exercise 5**

In this exercise the aim is to work on depression. The importance of this exercise depends upon the extent to which you become depressed.

Depression should not be mistaken for negativity. You can readily be negative without being depressed. It is, of course, often true that the depressed person is also quite negative.

To understand depression fully it is important to realize that it acts on your three centres: your physical centre, your emotional centre, and your intellectual centre[4]. The Gurdjieffian system holds that depression is the state where all three centres lack energy.

Depression can arise as a result of your having a false picture of yourself. If you consider yourself successful and you are not, then you will become depressed: if you think you are young and beautiful and you are not, then you will become depressed; if you think you are fully in control of yourself and you are not, then you will become depressed. Alternatively it can develop out of a loss of hope and belief in the future. It is a mistake, however, to think that loss of hope and belief in the future are the only, if not the main, reasons for depression. The realization that you are not what you have led yourself to believe you are is a much more common reason for being depressed. The first part of this exercise is, then, meant to help you to understand the causes of your depression.

Once you recognize the depression, the next step in the exercise is to make a tremendous effort to overcome it. You do this by putting a lot of effort into doing something, and doing this something consciously. To take a trivial example, suppose you are depressed. As you know, depression saps your energy. But energy is there for you to use, so long as you apply conscious effort. Make a decision then to rearrange all of your furniture, or to wash all the cupboards in the kitchen or clear out the attic. It does not matter what it is so long as you apply *conscious effort* to the task. It is this conscious effort which will lift you out of your depression. In the longer term, depression will only be reduced by not having a false picture of yourself and raising your overall level of energy by engaging in non-attachment.

## Exercise 6

In the Gurdjieffian system worry is considered as a form of 'inner identifying', a combination of one's imagination at work and some actual information. More succinctly, the imagination makes incorrect use of the facts, and it is this which creates worry. It is a negative state, a state of self-justification. Worry is different from thinking in a conscious way, because the worry is the driving force. As a result worry leads to a loss of force, a feature we commonly feel but tend to ignore. This gives us a clue of how to overcome worry. It is necessary to behave and think *consciously*. We must think clearly and formulate definite aims and objectives.

## Exercise 7

This exercise is simple to state but not easy to do. The very fact that it is not easy illustrates the strong hold certain behaviour has over the way we think and behave. The object is to avoid negative talk, to stop criticizing others, telling tales, engaging in spreading gossip about other people.

The first part of this exercise is simply to observe yourself doing these things. Notice how easy it appears to be, and most especially note that when in company how simple it is for a group to be sucked into such comments. When you criticize people (usually not to their face), consider what thought processes you go through. Attempt to criticize yourself from the same point of view! Criticism of others is really a way of giving importance to yourself, to your false personality. In order, then, to stimulate essence and reduce the influence of personality it is necessary to avoid engaging in negative conversations of this kind, and always to be as consciously aware as you can of exactly what you say. Your conversation should never be thoughtless, a mere mechanical response.

## Exercise 8

This exercise is an adaptation and elaboration of that suggested in *The Cloud of Unknowing*. It was there suggested that a word or phrase such as *god* or *love* could be fixed deep in one's consciousness and called on whenever 'incorrect' thoughts entered one's mind. This is a very simple but effective suggestion. The first problem is to choose the right word or phrase – your *mantra*. It should have these properties:

1. it should be short – one word is better than a phrase;
2. the word should have a powerful connotation, with a great deal of meaning for you personally; and
3. you should be capable of summoning up a vivid and creative image whenever the word is invoked.

In *The Cloud of Unknowing* the words *god* and *love* were suggested. Another common word used by Westerners is *Jesus*[5]; or the word could even be the name of a saint. These are typically Christian mantras.

The choice of mantra is important because as the word is used constantly over time a person becomes committed to and identified with it. This is especially true if a creative image is simultaneously invoked. It is fairly clear that the

word must have a powerful personal connotation.
Whether *god, Jesus, love,* or some other word entirely is
used depends on you. The first two have clear religious
connotations. The third word can have a religious
connotation but not necessarily.

The third property, that of summoning up a creative
image[6], may be the most difficult of all, especially if you
choose *god* or *love* for your mantra, because these are rather
abstract concepts. It is difficult here to make any
suggestion since your choice of a visualization must be
particular to you. However, if you are having difficulty,
then reading the works of St Teresa of Avila will give you
some guidance, as will the texts of St John of the Cross.

Assuming now that you have a mantra and can conjure
up an image when thinking of it, how do you then use this
technique? The solution is quite simple. Each time you
have a thought which is negative or involves an attachment
you simply think about the word and its accompanying
visual image. So long as this word and all it means to you
is in your consciousness then there will be no room for
thoughts about any attachment or negativity.

You will notice that there is an attachment here: namely,
to the mantra and what it means. The difference is that you
*choose* this particular attachment. This, of course, is the
basis of the techniques for meditating. In meditation you
concentrate on an idea. As other thoughts enter your head,
as they inevitably will, you simply bring your concentration back to the object on which you are meditating. In
the present case, however, the difference is that the word
is used as an aid in correct thinking. Because it is used
thus, as a piece of armour to protect you from negative or
unproductive thoughts, then it can be used at any time and
any place. That it is all 'mental' means, that no one even
need know that you are invoking this word and image.

As with a number of the exercises we shall be developing

here, the simplicity of this one should not be equated with ineffectiveness. If anything, the reverse is true: the more simple the more effective.

## Exercise 9

This exercise is also adapted from *The Cloud of Unknowing*. One technique of modern behaviour therapy is to carry out some unwanted behaviour to excess: to such an excess that you no longer want to do it. In other words, you create a surfeit of it to such an extent that you react against it. Thus, if you have a liking for a particular food which is not good for you, such as chocolate, then you eat it all the time until you cannot stand the sight of it.

Now the same technique, adapted somewhat, can be used in achieving non-attachment. You imagine (or carry out) the effects of your attachment over and over again until you are so absorbed in the attachment that you just wish it would go away. At this point you bring into your consciousness the full impact of the attachment and the futility of all it entails. You bring yourself to the point of humiliation, realizing at the same time that the very thing which is bringing you to this point of humiliation is the attachment which you have. If strong enough, this will provide you with the force for breaking the attachment. No one likes being utterly humiliated, even in the mind's eye. However, only if the humiliation is complete will the force be strong enough to break the attachment.

## Exercise 10

The impetus behind this next exercise runs through most Christian writings and has full expression in the life of Jesus. *You must have no high opinion of yourself but always think highly of others*. This does not mean that you should hate yourself. Christ did not hate himself. The point being emphasized is that if you have no high opinion of yourself you are not attached to your personality: you do not feed your personality and create an inflated ego. Of course, there is always a tendency to act in a certain way but claim that you do not have a high opinion of yourself but are, rather, acting and behaving 'realistically'. The claim of being realistic is only an excuse for you to continue doing what you have always done, and hence for retaining the attachment which you are strongly denying exists.

## Exercise 11

The theme of this exercise also runs through most Christian writings. Establish a list of the things which you do *not* like doing, so you are fully aware of what they are. Whenever any of these things or circumstances arise, make strenuous efforts not to give in to your inclinations. Life throws up so many of these that there will be ample opportunity throughout any given day to practise this exercise. Take just a trivial example. Laziness is common because human nature is such that it takes the path of least resistance. Giving in to laziness is always the path of least resistance. That this is so obviously true is borne out when one tries to overcome it. To overcome laziness requires effort, it requires a struggle with your personality, it requires that you become embroiled in a yes/no conflict. Thus, the moment you are faced with something and are about to ignore it because it involves effort, then this is the very time you should make a sincere effort. Notice that in doing this you *consciously* decide to do what your nature is trying to tell you not to do: It is a positive conscious act.

But laziness is not the only occasion when this exercise can be used. Being told to do something by someone else often leads us not to do what is asked. Why is this? It is because our ego is offended. When we have a high regard for ourselves then we do not like being told to do something by someone else because that places us below the other person, we perceive it as making us 'less important' than the other person. It is necessary, however, to do the things we are asked to do without begrudging the fact. It is not simply a question of doing the job, it must be done willingly and without complaint (verbal or mental) otherwise the ego is still being inflated.

As I have said, in any given day there are very many opportunities to practise this exercise. Although it is simple to state it is far from easy to accomplish. It requires constant practice. The reason it is so difficult is understandable: In order to accomplish this in all things requires humility. If you find this exercise very difficult, then take note of what some of the writers quoted throughout this book have said. And start with little things. Overcome little acts of laziness. Through these little victories you will save force, and in saving force you will be able to overcome greater things.

## Exercise 12

One of the great weaknesses human beings have is that of finding fault with others. This is no more than giving importance to the self, of giving sustenance to the ego. One important exercise to combat this trait is to try to refrain from finding trifling (or not so trifling) faults in others. There is a great tendency, especially when people are gathered together in groups, for one person to point out a fault in another (usually not someone present at the time!), and very soon the whole group is finding fault with that person. Either refrain from finding fault or refuse to contemplate such a fault. If necessary consider the person's good points. Another method, suggested by St Teresa, is that of keeping silent. In other words, when in a group do not contribute to the general negative and destructive discussion. If possible try to change the subject.

If fault finding with others occurs even when you are alone with your private thoughts, then use Exercise 8 to overcome them. Bring your chosen mantra into consciousness and so banish from your mind all negative and destructive thoughts.

### Exercise 13

This exercise is an adaptation of that suggested by St John of the Cross (p. 140). Aim to have a *habitual* desire to imitate someone of great goodness. This may be Christ, Buddha, one of the saints or simply a person you know who possesses obvious goodness[7]. It is better to fix on just one person because you can then identify with him or her more completely[8]. This identification will become more meaningful the more you know about the person. Therefore, part of this exercise involves finding out as much as you can about your chosen person. Try to find out as much as you can about him or her, and, most especially, try to know how he or she reacted to and spoke about different situations. Note to what extent he or she refrained from taking the easy route (remembering that the easy route is a way of giving in to the ego). Find out about the conflicts – inner and outer – that the person faced, and most especially how he or she dealt with them. The aim is not only to imitate your chosen role model but to have a *habitual* desire to imitate him or her. Once it becomes habitual you will not have to think consciously about it – you will automatically behave in a manner similar to that of the person you admire.

### Exercise 14

This exercise is also an adaptation of that suggested by St

John of the Cross (p. 140), being his third recommendation for conquering the appetites. It is made up of a series of things to do:

1. Incline yourself not to the easiest of tasks but to the hardest.

   Not only will this help to break attachments, but it will also engage you in yes/no conflicts and so help you to develop your essence.

2. Incline yourself not to the most delightful but to the harshest.

   This will involve struggle and yes/no conflicts.

3. Incline yourself not to the most gratifying but to the less pleasant.

   This will make you humble and will inevitably involve you in inner conflict with your ego.

4. Incline yourself not to the highest and most precious (especially of possessions) but to the lowest and most despised.

5. Incline yourself to wanting nothing.

   The wanting of something is merely an expression of a particular attachment. Recognize it for what it is and deny it.

All these pursuits involve a denial of self and a subjugation of the ego. Furthermore, they must be engaged in *consciously* to be effective. Although they are easy to state, they are not easy to enact. This in itself should be thought about when attempting this exercise. Why are some tasks difficult and others easy? Why is pleasure sought and hardship shunned? Why is self-gratification easier than doing unpleasant things? Why is concerning yourself with the poor, the ill or drop-outs much more difficult than dealing with the successful or popular individual? Finally, why is it so difficult to want nothing no matter where one is in life?

**End Notes**

1. Another example of this phenomenon is when you put something away when you are drunk only to find when you are sober again that you cannot remember where it is – only when you are again drunk do you remember where you put it. This feature is discussed in detail in neurolinguistic programming (NLP) – see J. Grinder and R. Bandler, *Trance-formations*, (Real People Press, 1981) and E.L. Rossi, *The Psychobiology of Mind-Body Healing*, (W.W. Norton & Company, 1986). NLP gives some scientific support to the view that individuals are many 'I's'. Also see J. Glover, *I: The Philosophy and Psychology of Personal Identity*, (Penguin, 1989) for other evidence.

2. In the Gurdjieffian system, false personality is defined as the mental construct of 'I', which is not real; it is what we think ourselves to be. False personality is counter to any form of self-development (see p. 178 for further discussion).

3. See this author's *Creative Visualization*, (Thorsons, 1984).

4. See Chapter 1, the section entitled 'Emotional and Intellectual Awareness' (p. 36) and Chapter 2, the section entitled 'Gurdjieff's System' (p. 54).

5. The word *Jesus* is a mantra used by a number of religious groups.

6. On the topic of creative imagery, see this author's *Creative Visualization*, (Thorsons, 1984).

7. If you do not wish to consider a religious person, someone like Albert Schweitzer is the type of person I have in mind.

8. Note again that this is a *conscious* identification and not an unconscious one.

# Appendix: A Psychological Commentary on Non-attachment

What is quite striking when considering the works discussed in this book and comparing them with academic works on psychology is the divergence between the conception of the self and the role of the ego in human development. In order to make this divergence clear it will be useful first to outline what psychologists have to say about personality, and most especially about the 'ego' and the 'self'. These are of course vast topics, and we shall not go into the minute details of them here. My aim is more specific; it is to illustrate that non-attachment requires a conception of self which is different from that discussed by modern psychologists but is none the less clearly spelled out in many religious and esoteric works[1]. There are some academics who are coming round to this esoteric view of self[2]. But in order to make this clear it will be necessary to outline the history of personality as given in the psychological literature.

## A BRIEF HISTORY AND OUTLINE OF THE THEORIES OF PERSONALITY

Behaviourism dominated psychology during the period 1918 – 1940[3]. Watson's main works on behaviouristic psychology had been written by 1920, and his attack on introspection and the study of mental constructs received general and growing support from both psychologists and philosophers. Behaviourism culminated in the work of Skinner and his investigations into operant conditioning (reflex responses). Although there were other developments in psychology between the wars, they were largely confined to experimental research.

There was, however, work going on outside of the behaviourist paradigm, most especially that concerning human attitudes and studies made of basic human traits. Although these studies supplied data on human behaviour, they did not fit well into the typical experimental work which dominated contemporary academic scholarship. This 'fringe' research tended to be sporadic and designed to deal with specific problems. There were, however, enough studies to tempt some scholars into surveying and analysing them.

The main problem with behaviourism, and other similar studies, was that the individual as a whole entity was not being considered. Although it was true that some psychologists, for example William James and G. Stanley Hall, had insisted on a study of the whole personality, more 'divisive' studies had survived, particularly in the psychoanalytic movement pioneered by Freud, Jung and Adler. Their views at the time, however, were not accepted by all psychologists.

It is necessary to begin with the theories of Freud, the chief proponent of the psychoanalytic movement. Freud's theory of personality is that it is tripartite: consisting of the *id*, the *ego* and the *superego*. The id is made up of instinctive drives, such as hunger, thirst and the sexual urge. It involves a force whose purpose is to preserve life; it also seeks pleasure. Unfortunately, the id is constantly in a state of tension and seeks to reduce this tension by having its needs satisfied. The id is also impatient and wants its needs satisfied immediately. Thus the id is self-centred, avaricious and demands immediate gratification. According to Freud the greatest conflict comes from the sexual drive, from the *libido*. However, another major source of conflict comes from society, whose basic aim is for the general good. Because the individual and society have different aims, and because society is more powerful than the individual, then the id needs to be controlled. It is the major task of parents to place controls on their developing child's id. It is their role to create within the child, according to Freud, the superego. It is the superego which provides a sense of guilt when antisocial behaviour is practised.

Between the id and the superego lies the ego. The ego acts as a mediating force which seeks to maintain a balance between the internal drives of the id and the controlling force of the superego. Thus, life in these terms is made up of our psyche's continual attempts to maximize instinctual gratification while minimizing punishment and guilt.

Two principles dominate human behaviour. There is the *pleasure principle* and the *reality principle*. It is the id which works according to the pleasure principle, i.e., it seeks to avoid pain and obtain pleasure regardless of external considerations. It wants immediate satisfaction. The ego, on the other hand, works in accordance with the reality principle, i.e., images are tested against reality and, if necessary, bodily needs and functions delayed until the appropriate environmental conditions are obtained. Finally, the superego works in response to our conception of punishment and guilt.

But how does the individual maximize instinctual gratification of the id while minimizing punishment and guilt? Also, what role has the reality principle in this conflict? The answers lie in the concept of *defence mechanisms*. These defence mechanisms keep unwelcome thoughts and actions hidden, from both others and ourselves. Defence mechanisms keep unwanted thoughts buried deep in the unconscious mind, while allowing them some form of socially acceptable outlet.[4] Defence mechanisms are considered a necessary and essential part of living. Because the ego involves the reality principle, then these defence mechanisms aim to keep as close to reality as possible while at the same time always seeking to gratify the instincts[5]. This theory, only sketchily outlined here, has been the precursor of many others and is influential to this day.

However, towards the end of the 1930s in the United States there was an attempt to systematize the vast data from clinical psychologists working in a number of areas – such as social psychology, educational psychology, and industrial psychology. It was hoped that these studies would lead to the establishment of some general principles of personality. One of the earliest of these was G.W. Allport's *Personality: A Psychological Interpretation* (see the Bibliography). Allport's theory involved the basic concept of 'trait'. This, and other similar works, led the way to a personality-orientated psychology. The 'trait approach' to personality asserts that personality structure is something we all have in common, lying along dimensions such as extroversion-introversion or field dependence-independence, but also allowing differences between individuals according to their particular combination of traits. A typical modern exponent of this view is Eysenck, who extended the concepts of introversion-extroversion first introduced by Jung, and added to these other traits, for example, stable-unstable, which could appear within an individual in combination with other traits.

It is not surprising that the Freudian theory of personality and the trait theory of personality were rejected by some psychologists. A different and phenomenological approach to personality (i.e., fulfilment theories) saw the healthy growth of the individual as an expression of a great force within that individual. While Freud's theory implied conformity with the aims of society so as to avoid conflict, the fulfilment theories argue that the aim of the individual is to transcend society. Accordingly, an individual is supposed to develop imagination, self-reliance, and characteristics which allow him or her to discover new things about the self.

In fulfilment theories the notion of self assumes considerable significance, as for example in the 'client-centred' approach of Carl Rogers (the founder of this school). In personality research, phenomenological subjective experience is at the centre of any approach. Rogers' theory has three components: the *organism*, the *phenomenal field* and the *self*. In this the individual has both a biological and a Gestalt element. In such theories, not only are present and past experiences important, but also the personal meaning which an individual ascribes to these experiences. What matters, then, is the individual's perception of reality, and not the reality itself.

An alternative fulfilment theory is provided by Maslow, who sees the individual as composed of two complementary forces: one set ensures one's survival while the other is the push towards realizing one's potential, i.e., the *self-actualizing* force. Maslow considers that the self-actualizing force can only come into operation if the other basic physiological needs are first satisfied[6]. Although Maslow does not talk of self or ego, it is clear that each plays a part within his system.

The latest theories of personality are the cognitive theories which involve the process of self-understanding (a cognitive faculty). In personal construct theory, which originated with George Kelly, emphasis is placed on the compatibility of various aspects of the personality. Each individual has a cognitive construct of the world and of the self which makes up his or her personality. In this theory the individual is treated as a problem-solver whose aim is to eliminate inconsistency, since any inconsistency gives rise to an uncomfortable state of tension and anxiety. Contrary to Freud's view, cognitive theory argues that the individual does not erect defences but rather is prepared to modify his or her inner network of constructs when present ones fail to explain accurately what is being observed and experienced.

Nearly all theories hold that the personality grows and develops as the individual matures. This is expressed most particularly in Erikson's theory, which sees the personality grow through the steady integration of the individual (or ego, in Erikson's terms). His theory is a social theory of ego development rather than a biological one[7].

Although we have not done justice to any of the theories outlined here, it is hoped that what this discussion has provided is a sense of the way psychologists have perceived personality and the extent to which the ego is part of it. What does seem to be commonly agreed is that personality grows as a person matures. Psychologists see maturity as a development of the ego and as an expression of personality. Maturity is seen as a result of developing personality – of developing ego integrity, to use Erikson's term. But the works we have been discussing in this book do not seem to be talking the same language! In the first place, they appear to be working with a different definition of self. Second, they stress the *subjugation* of the ego, the subjugation of personality. In order to get to grips with the difference it is necessary first to outline in some detail the Gurdjieffian view of essence and personality. Not only is this one of the clearest expressions of the esoteric view of personality, but it provides a basis upon which to

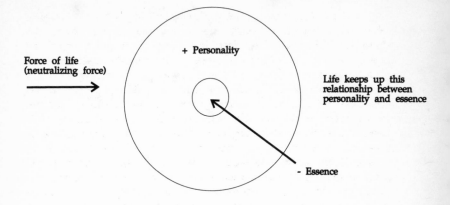

Force of life
(neutralizing force)

+ Personality

Life keeps up this
relationship between
personality and essence

- Essence

Figure 3(a)

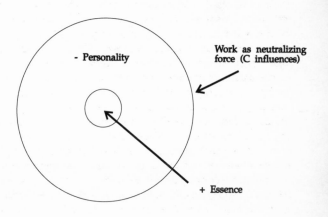

- Personality

Work as neutralizing
force (C influences)

+ Essence

Figure 3(b)

*Figure 3*  Essence and Personality

compare its view with those of the psychologists.

## THE GURDJIEFFIAN VIEW OF ESSENCE AND PERSONALITY

Each of us is born with *essence*, which grows for a brief time, until we
are about the age of three or four. From about the age of four *personality*

grows around essence. Essence, then, is what remains after personality is removed. Essence is the true person, but is separated from personality. As personality grows it becomes active (shown in Figure 3(a) by a positive symbol) while essence becomes passive (shown in Figure 3(a) by a negative symbol).

These two forces are kept in balance in this way by life, which acts as the neutralizing force[8]. Besides knowledge of the system, there is the aim of 'the Work', i.e., the acquisition of knowledge about the self and the means of changing being. This change of being is accomplished by changing the polarity between personality and essence: to make essence positive and personality passive, as illustrated in Figure 3(b). But before this can happen it is necessary for personality to grow to a sufficient level. It is essential, then, that life's forces act on us and that we form our personality sufficiently as a consequence. The reason for this is that development of essence must come about through personality: essence must *learn* from personality.

Unfortunately, it is also at this stage that 'false personality' develops. False personality is the mental construct of 'I', which is not real; it is what we imagine ourselves to be. False personality is counter to any form of self-development; it prevents self-development by creating 'buffers' which in turn keep us from seeing the truth about ourselves and other things. In particular, buffers prevent us from seeing how contradictory we are as we shift from one 'I' to another. When we are one particular 'I', in one compartment as it were, we think this is our whole being; but when we shift to another 'I', to another compartment, then once again this is our whole being. The fact that the second may be inconsistent with the first never enters our consciousness, because the buffer prevents it from doing so[9].

What is done by personality is done through external circumstance. In other words, we simply respond to life's influences. We learn from them, react to them and develop a personality to cope with them. We develop the 'I' which responds to life's circumstances. This, however, is the 'I' of our personality, and *not* the true, inner 'I' which belongs to essence. But it is in developing this concept of 'I' that we develop our 'false personality'[10]. So long as we consider the personality to be our essential 'I' we will not look for the true, inner 'I'[11].

Although the aim is to reverse the polarity between essence and personality as shown in Figure 3(b), the problem is how to accomplish this. It was noted above that life acts as the neutralizing force which maintains the polarity between essence and personality, as indicated in Figure 3(a). There is, then, another force required to help reverse this polarity. In the Gurdjieffian system this is provided by *C-influences*[12].

The C-influence is a new knowledge: the esoteric teaching of the Work. The problem is that we do not possess this force ourselves. It must come from outside ourselves, and it is necessary for us to make contact with it. The difficulty lies in knowing how to make this contact. It is made through effort, through the process of non-identifying – i.e., the process of non-attachment.

Positive and negative ideas in Gurdjieff's system are defined in a specific way. Anything that develops the false personality is negative. Negative ideas, which develop the false personality, can never lead to the individual's inner growth, to the development of essence. Positive ideas, unfortunately, require new knowledge, and new knowledge cannot be obtained from life's influences. Life's influences simply develop personality (and possibly false personality) further. In terms of the Work,

> To change things, to change his life, a man must first change himself. And in order to change himself he must find a teaching that will tell him how to do so. He must be willing to be taught new knowledge, new truth, and to begin to think in a new way. If he continues to think from the knowledge he has acquired, he will continue to think in the old way and then nothing can change. Only thinking in a new way can change a man. [13]

A fundamental positive idea, therefore, is essential if you wish to change yourself.

The sequence of events should be clearly understood. Essence grows very briefly in the first three or four years of life and then stops as personality develops around it. Personality becomes active while essence becomes passive, and this polarity is maintained by life's forces. It is, however, necessary to develop a rich personality. This is because when the time is right and esoteric teaching (which provides the force necessary to reverse the polarity between personality and essence) is acquired, then essence can grow. Essence can grow by making the personality passive. While passive the personality allows whatever is valuable in it to be transmitted to essence, thus does essence grow. So long as the individual identifies with things, has attachment to things, then personality is active, and so long as personality is active essence cannot grow.

## A COMMENTARY

Two things are striking about the comments made so far. First, there is a great difference between the discussion of ego and self in the psychological literature and that in the esoteric literature, here exemplified by the system laid out by Gurdjieff. Second, although the religious works discussed in this book do not go into any detail about the ego and the self, it is quite clear that they speak of the personality, for how else can we interpret such phrases as 'being dead of self'? We can use the system of Gurdjieff to interpret these religious works. All of them say that personality must become passive, and that a person must achieve non-attachment, for only by so doing will personality become passive, and only then can a person know his or her true self, only then can a person know his or her essence. More than that, only by so doing can work on essence begin.

Having spent many years developing the personality, it is clear that it will not be a simple task making the personality passive, when it has, as it were, been in the driver's seat for so long.

The religious works also seem to agree that a force outside of oneself is required to help reverse the polarity and make personality passive and essence positive. What exactly this is, and how it can be called upon, is to a large extent where the treatises differ. But they only differ in detail. Non-attachment is the common thread running through all these works. But to achieve non-attachment it is necessary to know thyself. What is being advocated here is a process of looking inward rather than simply responding mechanically to life's conditions.

Furthermore, there is general agreement that the path is not one of changing life's conditions, but rather of changing oneself. Here we come to the two important statements made so clearly by St John of the Cross[14]:

> To come to the knowledge you have not
> you must go by a way in which you know not.

and

> To come to be what you are not
> you must go by a way in which you are not.

We see over and over again the statement that if you change outside circumstances all you are doing is changing the way life influences your personality; what you do *not* do is alter your essence. You can only alter essence by creating a magnetic centre from which influences flow outward from within yourself to the outside world.

This is made very clear by St Teresa of Avila. In her life story we have a full expression of the difficulties one person encountered in suppressing personality and making it passive; of not only allowing essence to grow, but ensuring that it grew.

Let us, however, return to the psychological works on personality.

Some represent no more than a scientist's aim to classify and distinguish aspects of a person's psychological make-up. But one outgrowth of self-actualizing models of personality is to develop fully the meaning of self. However, in terms of the Gurdjieffian system, the only thing these models help the individual doing is to develop the personality, and false personality at that. They in no way lead to an understanding of essence. In these terms, the claim that self-actualization leads to an appreciation of the true self is misdirected. All self-actualization does is give one a deeper understanding of the false personality.

The same is true of other approaches to personality, such as the cognitive theories of personality. As problem-solvers, all they help a person do is to respond to life's conditions. Until the individual chooses to take a *new* route, there can be no understanding of his or her true self.

This argument should not be taken too far, however. Gurdjieff insisted that personality must grow before it is made passive. Self-actualization may be no more than a means of developing a good and fruitful personality, from which essence can eventually learn. In this sense, *there is no conflict between ego development and non-attachment*. There will only be conflict if ego development is continued while the individual attempts to achieve non-attachment.

What is lacking in the psychological theories of personality outlined above is an awareness that eventually one needs to make the personality passive. But this is understandable, since this would take psychology out of the realm of science and into the realm of religious thought and philosophy. So long as scientists refuse to go that extra step they will fail in the ultimate purpose of their pursuit of knowledge.

## A SOCIETY BASED ON CO-OPERATION

The development of personality, whether from the point of view of psychologists or from the point of view of Gurdjieff, means that an individual tends to be self-centred. This is because personality, in terms of the id, desires immediate gratification. In Freudian terms the personality is only circumvented from this by the superego, which takes account of society's aims. The superego is, however, still part of personality as interpreted within the Gurdjieffian system. The same is true of Erikson's final stage of development in terms of ego integrity. It is also true of cognitive theories of personality, since in this case society simply throws up different problems for the individual to solve.

We are basically egocentric and consequently there is a tendency towards conflict within any group situation. Fritjof Capra in his book

*The Turning Point* (Fontana, 1982) argues that a new conception of man can be expressed in terms of systems theory: what he calls a 'systems view of life'. This is part of the holistic movement that is becoming more and more dominant a feature of today's world. His theory holds that organisms have hierarchical structures, in which parts co-operate for the benefit of the whole. It is not my intention here to develop this argument further, all I wish to point out is that when individuals achieve non-attachment they stop being egocentric and look to the benefit of society as a whole. It is the ego which leads to conflict; a person 'dead of self' will not engage in such conflict since there is no point in it. The ego is a negative influence and not a positive one. A non-attached person is only interested in positive influences. Unfortunately, since so few individuals have achieved a state of non-attachment, then a fully co-operative society seems at the moment a long way off. Be this as it may, every individual attempt at non-attachment will bring society closer to this goal.

## End Notes

1. More detailed information on the psychological treatment of self, as well as of other psychological ideas as discussed in this Appendix, can be found in the following texts:
   C.J. Adcock, *Fundamentals of Psychology*, (Pelican, 1964).
   H.J. Eysenck, *Sense and Nonsense in Psychology*, (Pelican, 1957).
   B.M. Foss (ed.), *New Horizons in Psychology*, (Pelican, 1966).
   Sigmund Freud, *Two Short Accounts of Psycho-Analysis*, (Pelican, 1962).
   P. Lloyd *et al.*, *Introduction to Psychology*, (Fontana, 1984).
   G.A. Miller, *Psychology*, (Pelican, 1966).
   W. Mischel, *Introduction to Psychology*, (Holt, Rinehart and Winston, 2nd ed., 1976).
   R. Thomson, *The Pelican History of Psychology*, (Penguin, 1968).
2. See J. Glover, *I: The Philosophy and Psychology of Personal Identity*, (Penguin, 1989).
3. This account draws in part on R. Thomson's work, *The Pelican History of Psychology*, (Penguin, 1968).
4. The form of outlet depends on the type of defence mechanism involved. They include: projection, denial, reaction formation, regression, rationalization and sublimation.
5. It is possible to argue that this approach gives a psychological basis for the *buffers* discussed in the Gurdjieffian system, as considered on pages 160 and 178.
6. Maslow's theory is based on a hierarchical system of needs. At the top of this hierarchy is the need for self-actualization.

7. Erikson's theory involves eight psycho-social stages of development. His view is that individuals must overcome a number of crises in order to achieve full maturity.

8. Gurdjieff's system stresses the importance of the third force, such as the neutralizing force of life or C-influences. These third forces are ignored by present-day science.

9. Buffers are an important part of the Gurdjieffian system and also give major insight into non-attachment. However, to understand fully the role played by buffers it is necessary to understand the Gurdjieffian system in more detail. See P.D. Ouspensky, *The Fourth Way*, (Routledge & Kegan Paul, 1957) and *In Search of the Miraculous*, (Routledge & Kegan Paul, 1950); also see Maurice Nicoll, *Psychological Commentaries on the Teachings of G.I. Gurdjieff and P.D. Ouspensky*, 3 vols., (Watkins, 1952).

10. It is a 'false personality' because the 'I' which we develop is considered by us to be in some sense our true self when it is not; it considers itself to be the unchanging, permanent thing called 'I' when it is not.

11. This is one reason why ancient wisdom is often ignored. If you think you already have something, then when offered it you will refuse, thinking it is already in your possession!

12. In the Gurdjieffian system there are three types of influences on the individual, denoted A, B and C.

    A-influences are those from 'mechanical' life, the influences from everyday living. B-influences do not arise from life, they arise from religious texts, parables, fairy-tales, Sufi sayings, etc. They have an impact at a deeper level of our being. The sayings of Christ are archetypal B-influences.

    The sources of B-influences, however, are C-influences. These are explained rather vaguely. Ouspensky says they are influences we obtain by meeting with a person or group which influences us in a way *different* to the way in which we are affected by A- or B-influences. B-influences allow an individual to develop a magnetic centre. Once this centre is formed, then when the individual meets a person or group with C-influence he or she will have taken the first important step towards change and development.

    According to Ouspensky, C-influences can only come as a result of direct contact.

13. Nicoll, *Commentaries*, vol. 3, p. 1115.

14. *The Collected Works of St John of the Cross*, translated by Kieran Kavanaugh and Otilio Rodriguez © 1979 by Washington Province of Discalced Carmelites. ICS Publications, 2131 Lincoln Road, N.E., Washington, D.C. 20002, U.S.A., p. 103.

# Bibliography

Adcock, C.J., *Fundamentals of Psychology*, (Pelican, 1964).

Allport, G.W., *Personality: A Psychological Interpretation*, (Holt, Rinehart and Winston, 1937).

Assagioli, R., *Psychosynthesis*, (Turnstone Books, 1975).

Bennett, J.G., *Witness: The Autobiography of John Bennett*, (Turnstone Books, 1974).

Benson, H., *The Relaxation Response*, (Fount Paperbacks, 1977).

– -, *Beyond the Relaxation Response*, (Fount Paperbacks, 1985).

Berne, E., *Games People Play*, (Penguin, 1966).

Capra, Fritjof, *The Turning Point*, (Fontana, 1982).

Cox, M., *A Handbook of Christian Mysticism*, (The Aquarian Press, 1986).

Drury, Neville, *Don Juan, Mescalito and Modern Magic*, (Arkana, 1985).

Eysenck, H.J., *Sense and Nonsense in Psychology*, (Pelican, 1957).

Foss, B.M. (ed.), *New Horizons in Psychology*, (Pelican, 1966).

Freud, Sigmund, *Two Short Accounts of Psycho-Analysis*, (Pelican, 1962).

Glover, J., *I: The Philosophy and Psychology of Personal Identity*, (Penguin, 1989).

Grinder, J. and Bandler, R., *Trance-formations*, (Real People Press, 1981).

Gurdjieff, G.I., *Beelzebub's Tales to His Grandson*, (Routledge & Kegan Paul, 1950).

– -, *Meetings with Remarkable Men*, (Picador, 1978).

– -, *Life is Real Only Then, When 'I Am'*, (Routledge & Kegan Paul, 1981).

– -, *Views from the Real World*, (Arkana, 1984).

Hilton, W., *The Ladder of Perfection*, translated by Leo Shirley-Price, (Penguin, 1957).

Huxley, Aldous, *The Perennial Philosophy*, (Triad Grafton Books, 1985).

Jacobson, E., *You Must Relax*, (Unwin Paperbacks, 1980).

James, William, *The Varieties of Religious Experience*, (Penguin, 1982).

Johnston, William, *Silent Music*, (Fount Paperbacks, 1974).

– -, *The Mirror Mind*, (Fount Paperbacks, 1983).

Jung, C.G., *Man and His Symbols*, (Pan Books, 1978).

Kavanaugh, Kieran and Rodriguez, Otilio (trs.), *The Collected Works of St John of the Cross*, (ICS Publications, 1979).

Kempis, Thomas à, *The Imitation of Christ*, translated by Betty I. Knott (HarperCollinsPublishers, 1983).

Lloyd, P., *et al.*, *Introduction to Psychology*, (Fontana, 1984).

Miller, G.A., *Psychology*, (Pelican, 1966).

Mischel, W., *Introduction to Psychology*, (Holt, Rinehart and Winston, 2nd edition, 1976).

*The New English Bible*, (Oxford University Press, 1970).

Nicoll, Maurice, *Psychological Commentaries on the Teachings of G.I. Gurdjieff and P.D. Ouspensky*, 3 vols., (Watkins, 1952).

Ouspensky, P.D., *A New Model of the Universe*, (Routledge & Kegan Paul, 1931).

– -, *In Search of the Miraculous*, (Routledge & Kegan Paul, 1950).

– -, *The Fourth Way* (Routledge & Kegan Paul, 1957).

– -, *The Psychology of Man's Possible Evolution*, (Arkana, 1991).

Rodriguez, Otilio and Kavanaugh, Kieran (trs.), *The Collected Works of St Teresa of Avila*, (ICS Publications, 1980).

Rossi, E.L., *The Psychobiology of Mind-Body Healing*, (W.W. Norton & Company, 1986).

St Ignatius Loyola, *The Spiritual Exercises of St Ignatius*, translated by A. Mottola, (Doubleday Image edition, 1989).

St Teresa of Avila, *The Life of Saint Teresa of Avila by Herself*, translated by J.M. Cohen, (Penguin, 1957).

Shah, Idries, *Tales of the Dervishes*, (Jonathan Cape, 1967).

Shone, Ronald, *Autohypnosis*, (Thorsons, 1982).

– -, *Creative Visualization*, (Thorsons, 1984).

Thomson, R., *The Pelican History of Psychology*, (Pelican, 1968).

Underhill, Evelyn, *Mysticism*, (Methuen, 15th edition, 1945)

Waldberg, M., *Gurdjieff: An Approach to His Ideas*, (Arkana, 1989).

Wolters, C. (tr.), *The Cloud of Unknowing and Other Works*, (Penguin, 1961).

Woods, R. (ed.), *Understanding Mysticism*, (The Athlone Press, 1981).

# Index